G000123826

THE
INTERNET GUIDE

Hands-On Global Networking

**Brent Heslop and
David Angell**

Addison-Wesley Publishing Company

Reading, Massachusetts ▪ Menlo Park, California ▪ New York
Don Mills, Ontario ▪ Wokingham, England ▪ Amsterdam
Bonn ▪ Sydney ▪ Singapore ▪ Tokyo ▪ Madrid ▪ San Juan
Paris ▪ Seoul ▪ Milan ▪ Mexico City ▪ Taipei

Library of Congress Cataloging-in-Publication Data
Heslop, Brent D.
    The instant Internet guide: hands-on global networking/Brent
    Heslop and David Angell.
        p.   cm.
    Includes index.
    ISBN 0-201-62707-8
    1. Internet (Computer network) I. Angell, David. II. Title.
TK5105.875.I57H48   1994
004.6'7- -dc20

                                                    93-33548
                                                    CIP

Sponsoring Editor: Phil Sutherland
Project Editor: Claire Horne
Production Coordinators: Vicki Hochstedler and Lora Ryan
Cover design: Jean Seal
Set in Meridien and Futura type by Editorial Services of New England, Inc.

1 2 3 4 5 6 7 8 9 -ARM- 9796959493
First printing December 1993

Addison-Wesley books are available for bulk purchases by corpora-tions, institutions, and other organizations. For more information please contact the Corporate, Government and Special Sales Department at (617) 944-3700 ×2915.

Contents

Chapter 3

Turning On Network News

Chapter 4

Interactive Internet

Chapter 5

Mining Files on the Internet

Chapter 6

Finding What You Want on the Internet 125

Chapter 7

UNIX in About an Hour 153

Appendix

Getting a Dial-up Connection to the Internet 191

Index 201

Acknowledgments

Writing this book was a fun-filled collaboration with a lot of special people who helped us on our Internet safari. We want to thank the following people for their help: Phil Sutherland at Addison-Wesley, who gave us the opportunity to write this book; Kimn Neilson, Jenny Kilgore, and Claire Horne, who policed our writing and kept us from reckless verbiage; and Steve Wertz and Dusty Smith for their detailed technical edits, which had them traveling the Internet at all hours.

We owe a huge debt of gratitude to Brian Fudge, Rene Gallagher, Rich White, and John Little at Portal Communications. They made our Internet travel first-class, answering our numerous questions and making sure we had access to the latest versions of Internet programs. Additional thanks to Brian Fudge for reviewing our manuscript. Desirree Madison-Biggs graciously opened up NETCOM's impressive Internet access services for our use during this project. We also want to express our appreciation to Robert Adams and Walt Howe at Delphi Communications, Suzanne Koumantzelis at HoloNet, Gail Ann Williams at The WELL, and Amy Arnold at America Online.

For helping us make the communication link to Internet service providers smooth, we want to thank Jeff Beamsley at Hilgraeve for HyperAccess for Windows, and Fritz Mueller and Donna Loughlin at NetManage for Chameleon.

As always, we want to thank our wives, Kim Merry and Joanne Angell, for putting up with yet another passionate book affair.

Read Me First

Before you get carried away with visions of William Gibson's *Neuromancer* Cyberspace dancing in your head, it's time for a reality check. Cybersurfing the Internet for the uninitiated can be a wipeout. *The Instant Internet Guide* teaches anyone how to catch the Internet wave, including the lone PC or Mac Internet surfer. Regardless of how you're connected to the Internet, *The Instant Internet Guide* delivers concise, hands-on techniques to make your Internet ride as fast and smooth as possible. We have chosen the friendliest and most widely available programs for performing Internet tasks. While the Internet is a sea of constantly changing programs, we have taken great pains to provide the most up-to-date information available.

To make our coaching instructions easier to follow, we use some simple conventions. Commands, program names, and keystrokes are in boldface. For example, to start the **pine** program, you are instructed to type **pine**. Anytime we tell you to press a key or keys in text, we bold the keys. When we tell you to press **Enter**, it means press the Enter or Return key on your keyboard. Most of the Internet is UNIX based, and UNIX is case sensitive, so when typing in command and examples be sure to match the case as shown. If you see an instruction to press a key combination, such as **Ctrl-C**, hold down the Control key and press the **C** key; don't press the hyphen between the two keys. Most Ctrl key combinations are not case sensitive, so you can use the lowercase characters.

New terms and variable input that you supply as part of performing a task (such as an e-mail address, a file name, or a computer address) are in italic, for example, **telnet** *host-computer-address*. Messages that appear on your screen are printed in a courier font, for example, `Press any key to continue`. Related supplementary information is noted as a **Tip**, **Caution**, or **FYI** (For Your Information).

If you have any comments about this guide, we invite you to send an e-mail message to either of us. Surf's up!

October 1993   Brent Heslop
                          bheslop@shell.portal.com

                          David Angell
                          dangell@shell.portal.com

Chapter 1

MERGING ONTO THE INTERNET

Just as the interstate highway system links cities to other cities, so the Internet links thousands of computer networks. The Internet is the mother of all networks. Born from the R & D demands of the military-industrial complex, it has become a quilted patchwork of more than 13,000 networks connecting over 15 million people. Before you merge onto this digital superhighway, read this chapter. Like a AAA guidebook, it guides you through the basics of cruising the Internet, including what the Internet is, access connections to the Internet, and how to login to the Internet. It also surveys the tools of the Internet traveler and explains the rules of the road for working and communicating on the Internet. There will be a quiz later!

PREPARING YOURSELF FOR THE INTERNET

The Internet is dominated by mainframe and minicomputers operated by large government, corporate, and educational institutions. It's a digital world populated by techno-weenies, hostile user interfaces, and barren text screen displays. Unlike commercial online services, the Internet isn't one centralized system. There is no one organization you can call to complain about the Internet. It's a network of networks, where every site is an island

governed by it's local tribal council or MIS (Management
Information Systems) department.

The media love to hype the Internet as the digital
highway of the future. But what they don't tell you is
that working on the Internet can take the patience
needed for driving in bumper-to-bumper traffic. As hap-
pens with highways, the more people use the Internet,
the more congested it becomes. Adding to your traveling
woes are the older, command-line software vehicles
used to cruise the Internet; however, sportier menu-
based and platform-specific graphical user interface
(GUI) programs are emerging.

There is a reason the Internet is crowded and contin-
ues to grow more so; it's a computer matrix filled with a
cornucopia of resources. These resources include people
from all walks of life, online databases and library card
catalogs, computing facilities, and files containing everything imaginable. Because of the Internet's connections
and resources, it's rapidly becoming a staple of modern
business communications. By 1998 the Internet is
expected to exceed 100 million users worldwide. Organizations and individuals around the world are setting
up shop on the Internet to conduct and deliver a wide
range of interactive online services. Learning to surf the
Internet is well worth the effort.

Internet Networking in a Nutshell

Networking is a simple concept that forms the basis of
the Internet. Simply stated, networking is the sharing of
resources among computer users. These resources consist of information, the computers themselves, and
human expertise. Rather than duplicate the resource at
many sites, the resource is centralized and can be
accessed by any user through connections between computers. These connections range from sophisticated,
high-speed fiber optic connections to the humble

modem. The fundamental structure of a relationship between two computers connected via the Internet is the *client/server* model. A *client* is any computer remotely connected to a host computer, called a *server*, to run programs via the network.

To connect different types of computers and transfer information successfully between them requires a standardized set of rules, called *protocols*. The Transmission Control Protocol/Internet Protocol (TCP/IP) is the glue that holds all the different computer systems together on the Internet. TCP/IP ensures data is routed correctly by defining the addresses used to send information across the Internet.

Internet Addresses

Every computer connected to the Internet has its own address, much like a postal address. The Internet address is as important as a postal address for sending letters. There are two main types of addresses on the Internet, *IP addresses* and *domain names*. Each computer that uses TCP/IP protocols is distinguished from other computers on the Internet by a unique IP address, also referred to as an *Internet address*. An IP address is four numbers separated by periods; for example, **129.32.1.100**. The pieces of the IP address separated by dots are hierarchical, with the leftmost numbers representing what network you're part of, followed by numbers representing the subnetwork, then the specific host or computer.

Domain Name System

Originally, computers connected on the Internet were identified only by their IP numeric addresses. IP numeric addresses can be difficult to remember, so a text system was developed called the *domain name system*. For the most part, domain names are chosen to be indicative of

the name and type of service and organization that owns
or supports the service. Domain names are organized in
a hierarchical fashion, as are IP addresses, except in
reverse order, with the most specific (computer name)
at the left to the most general, top-level domain to the
right. For example, **ames.arc.nasa.gov** indicates the
site is connected to a government domain account at
NASA. As you work with domain names, you'll become
adept at interpreting their source organizations and locations. The top-level domains on the Internet include the
following:

Domain	Organization
com	Commercial
edu	Educational
gov	Government
mil	Military
org	Other
net	Network resources
au	Country (Australia, in this example)

For most Internet services, either the domain name or
the IP address will work to reach a machine, but it's
better to stick with domain names. Not only is it easier
to remember a domain name, but IP addresses are tied
to specific networks. If the computer providing a service
is moved from one location to another, its network and
hence its address will change. The domain name doesn't
need to change. When the system administrator assigns
the new address, he or she only needs to update the
name record so that the name points to the new address.
Because the name still works, it doesn't matter if the
computer has changed locations.

Account IDs and User Names

Adding the address of an individual or account holder at a computer connected to the Internet for addressing electronic mail (e-mail) is fairly straightforward. The domain address is prefaced with the account ID or user name and the @ (at) symbol. For example, a user named Beavis at the domain name address shell.portal.com might have the e-mail address **beavis@shell.portal.com.** Institutions vary widely in the way they form account IDs or user names.

> **CAUTION:**   Don't guess someone's e-mail address. A message sent to an incorrect address unnecessarily adds to network traffic. Contact recipients before addressing your e-mail to get their correct e-mail addresses.

HOW ARE YOU ACCESSING THE INTERNET?

The three basic types of Internet connections are analogous to first class, business class, and coach. What class of access you have available to you determines the procedures you use to connect and work on the Internet. Here are the three ways you can connect to the Internet.

> **FYI:**   If you're not already connected to the Internet, see Appendix A for information on shopping for a service provider to connect to the Internet and a listing of major service providers.

First-Class Access: A Dedicated Connection

A dedicated connection is the first-class way to connect to the Internet. Traveling first class is expensive (we're talking thousands of dollars) and out of reach for the small business or individual PC or Mac user. This type of connection is standard fare, however, for most large corporations, academic institutions, and government organizations.

People who have direct connections are full-fledged Internet members. They don't have to worry about how much they use the Internet because the leased lines or network links are already paid for by the company or organization.

When you use a dedicated connection to the Internet, all you need is the account you already have to login to your local network. You can then login and start using the tools to access the Internet. Direct access operates much faster than other types of connections and lets you use programs that take advantage of the interface available at your site, such as friendlier GUI-based programs.

Business-Class Access: An Almost-Dedicated Connection

An almost-dedicated Internet connection allows a computer or small network of computers to become an Internet member with its own IP address, except there is an additional layer of complexity. This business-class type of Internet connection uses communications software for your particular computer that supports the Serial Line Internet Protocol (SLIP) or Point-to-Point Protocol (PPP) and a high-speed modem to connect to a service provider's computer. The service provider's computer acts as a conduit to connect a computer directly to the Internet over a telephone line.

Using a SLIP or PPP connection and a voice-grade or higher quality telephone line allows you to perform the full range of Internet tasks once you're connected to the service provider's computer. As with a full dedicated connection, you can use Internet tools that are based on your computer's operating system and GUI. It is not as fast as a full dedicated connection because there still is a modem link.

As the number of small businesses seeking to get connected to the Internet and the number of competing service providers grows, the SLIP and PPP are becoming increasingly viable options. While this business-class connection is considerably cheaper than a dedicated connection (usually under $200 a month), it's still out of reach for most individual PC or Mac users.

Coach-Class Access: Individual Dial-up Connections

The least expensive way to connect to the Internet for the rest of us individual PC and Mac users is by getting an account with a service provider. A service provider offers connections to the Internet through its computer system, which has a dedicated connection. You use a communications software package for your computer and a modem to dial up a service provider's computer that is directly connected to the Internet. Dial-up access doesn't let your computer be a part of the Internet directly; it's merely accessing a service provider's computer that is directly connected to the Internet. The service provider's computer, not your local computer, becomes the client computer when a connection to a remote computer is made.

This means that you have to deal with a service provider's computer system, which is usually a UNIX-based system, and you need to perform extra steps for some Internet tasks. For example, when you transfer a file from a host computer, it's transferred first to the service provider's computer. You then must transfer the file again, from the service provider computer to your computer, using your communications software.

> **TIP:** Your modem determines the speed with which you interact with the service provider. In modem communications, speed is everything. If you're working with a 2400-bps modem, upgrade if you can. The expense of buying a faster modem will quickly be paid back by money you save in hourly connection charges.

Shell and Menu Accounts. For individual dial-up connections, two main types of services are available for working on the Internet: shell accounts and menu accounts. The most common type of account on these computers is the shell account. A *shell* is the interface between you and the UNIX operating system; it translates commands you enter from the keyboard into code the operating system can understand. The shell account allows you to use a wide range of UNIX utilities to work on the Internet. Menu accounts are easier to use, but less versatile because you're usually tied to a menu system created by the access provider.

LOGGING INTO THE INTERNET

Logging into the Internet is your on-ramp to the Internet highway. It involves typing in your user name and password at the computer you're using to access the Internet. The system prompts you for your user name and password. If you make a mistake entering your user name or your password, try pressing **Ctrl-U** to delete the line and start over. In most cases, if you press **Backspace** when you login, a control code is sent as part of your entry and you will receive an error message asking you to reenter your user name or password. After you enter your password, you're logged into the computer and the Internet. You may be prompted to verify or choose a terminal emulation setting. Terminal emulation lets your computer connect to a host computer (server) by making your computer emulate a type of computer (terminal) with which the host can communicate. Whenever possible choose VT100. If you're using a Macintosh communications program that doesn't include the VT100 terminal emulation setting, choose VT102.

TIP: If strange or extra characters appear on your screen, check to make sure your communication program's terminal emulation setting matches the terminal emulation setting you chose when logging into your service provider account.

Your user name and password are determined when you establish an account, either by a system administrator for your local network or by the service provider. Your user name identifies you to the system and is also used for e-mail. Your user name is usually not a secret, so the only way you protect your account is with a password, which you can change.

Protecting Your Password

Your password protects you from other users taking unauthorized trips on the Internet at your expense. Most common security problems can be prevented if you are careful with your password. If an Internet hooligan, referred to as a *cracker*, gets your password and uses it to access your account uninvited, worse things can happen than just your files being looked at, modified, or deleted. The cracker in effect can use your name to post articles to newsgroups or mail messages. The results can be devastating. Here are guidelines for keeping your password a secret.

- Never give or e-mail anyone your password.
- If you open an account on another computer, don't use the same password that you use on your local computer.
- Be aware of others watching you login.
- Don't write your password down so others can see it.
- Be careful of anyone claiming by phone or e-mail to be a system administrator asking for your password. This could be a scam, much like con artists who try to get your credit card number over the phone.

Changing Your Password

Changing your password periodically helps keep your account secure. Most systems let you change your password. Different systems have different requirements for passwords. A password someone can easily guess is one of the most common causes of security breaches. Here are some guidelines to keep in mind when you create a new password.

- Never base a password on your own name, family member name, or pet name.
- Be creative. Pick a password that is easy to remember, yet not easily deduced by others.
- Don't use any word in the dictionary. Crackers often use online dictionaries to help break passwords.
- Make the password at least six characters and use a mixture of uppercase and lowercase letters, numbers, and other characters.
- Don't use a set of adjacent keyboard keys in a password.

Here are the steps to change your password on many service provider computers or other systems running UNIX.

1. At the system prompt, type **passwd.** The system responds with a prompt to enter your old password.
2. Enter your old password. When you enter your password, it's not displayed on the screen. The system prompts you for your new password.
3. Type your new password. The system then prompts you to reenter your new password for verification.
4. Enter your new password again. If you type a different password the second time, the system tells you there is a mismatch. You must then rerun the **passwd** program again.

YOUR UNIX HOME BASE

If you're connected to the Internet through a service provider's computer, chances are it's a UNIX-based computer. Your home base in a UNIX system is called your *home directory.* To start your Internet travels you don't need to work with UNIX commands right away. However, as you work on the Internet, you'll need to manage the files in your home directory using UNIX commands. Because UNIX is the common language of most computers connected to the Internet, learning common UNIX commands is like learning to speak some essential Spanish words before visiting Madrid.

> **FYI:** When you are ready to learn how to manage files in your home directory or learn some essential UNIX commands, see Chapter 7, UNIX in About an Hour.

TOOLS OF THE INTERNET TRAVELER

Once you login to a computer connected to the Internet, you're ready to start working with the tools of the Internet. Standard applications for working on the Internet are widely available and supported by most computers connected to the Internet. For many tasks there is more than one tool for getting the job done. Additionally, some of these tools are in the process of evolving from crude command-line programs to friendlier, menu-based programs. Here are the tools we have found most helpful.

Tool	Description
pine, mail, mailx	Sends, receives, and manages your e-mail communications. The **pine** program is a friendly, menu-based program. The **mail** and **mailx** programs are the older UNIX e-mail programs.

Tool	Description
tin	Reads and posts network news messages. Network news refers to ongoing discussions within interest groups. The **tin** program is a new generation of menu-based news reader program.
ftp	Transfers files between computers on the Internet.
telnet	Searches online resources, such as databases and library card catalogs.
archie, gopher, veronica, WAIS	Finds resources in the vast constellation of Internet computers.

LOGGING OUT OF THE INTERNET

Getting off the Internet involves logging out at the right exit. If you're using a computer that has a dedicated connection to the Internet, the procedure you use to logout of your local network logs you out of the Internet. If you're using a service provider, logging out of the Internet is a little more complicated. To logout of the Internet from a service provider, after exiting a tool at the system prompt, which is usually a $ or % symbol, type **exit.** Some service providers automatically disconnect you. Other service providers require you to type **exit** again to terminate the session or use an **exit** command from the communications software you're running on your local computer.

RULES OF THE INTERNET ROAD

Like any highway system, there are rules, restrictions, and policies that govern the actions of individual drivers for the common good of the Internet. Federal subsidies pay for large sections of the Internet in support of its research and education objectives. Because of this fact, what you can and can't do on the Internet is largely determined by the federal government. To determine what is acceptable use of the Internet, check with your service provider or system administrator for the rules, restrictions, and policies governing your connection to the Internet. Often these guidelines are posted for easy access. Beyond what is required, there is also a basic level of self-regulation in dealing with others on the Internet that falls within the category of Internet etiquette, commonly called *netiquette*.

Getting Directions

The Internet is well marked with information to help new travelers. Assistance to new users on the Internet comes in the form of files or messages for a variety of tools and services. The main form of help for new users are FAQs (Frequently Asked Questions), which are compiled lists of answers to common questions. The idea behind FAQs is to reduce potential problems and cut down on message traffic from new users asking the same questions. RFCs (Requests For Comments) are documents that detail procedures and provide general information. Generally RFCs are more technical in nature and not as useful for the average user. An FYI (For Your Information) document is like an RFC document but more introductory in nature.

Netiquette: Courtesy on the Road

Don't you hate the jerk who doesn't signal before switching lanes and cuts you off when you're driving down the highway. On the Internet, the instantaneous, informal qualities of electronic communications, plus the lack of tonal and visual cues, frequently lead to misunderstandings. The forms of electronic communications on the Internet include e-mail, posting articles to newsgroups, and online conferencing. This section provides netiquette guidelines for courteous electronic communications and tips for writing effective electronic communications. Remember, in electronic communications you are what you write.

Expressing Your Emotions with Smileys. A common problem with electronic communications is that it's easy to misinterpret a humorous or sarcastic message. A visual shorthand called *smileys* or *emoticons* has emerged to help convey the original intent of the author. Smileys are sideways faces created from keyboard characters that indicate an emotion. Hundreds of smileys have been created. They are usually placed after the sentence in question, for example

`See you at the company picnic.  ;-)`

Here is a list of popular smileys you can use in your messages to indicate a range of emotions.

Smiley	Emotion
:-)	Happy
:-(	Sad
:-&	Tongue-tied
:-<	Really upset!
:-||	Angry
:-@	Screaming
:-D	Laughing
;-)	Wink
:-}	Grin
8-)	Wide-eyed
:-|	Apathy
:-o	Shocked or amazed
:-]	Happy sarcasm or smirk
:-[	Sad sarcasm
;-(	Feel like crying
:'-(	Crying

Smiley	Emotion
%-)	Happy confused
%-(	Sad confused
:-*	Kiss
:-\	Undecided
:-#	My lips are sealed

> **FYI:** An extensive listing of smileys can be found via **ftp** at site: **nic.funet.fi,** directory: **/pub/doc/fun/misc,** file: **smiley.txt.gz.** See Chapter 5 for information on working with **ftp.**

Expressing emotions with written text isn't limited to smileys. Here are some other common shorthand expressions of emotion.

Shorthand	Emotion
<g>	Grin
<s>	Sigh
<l>	Laugh
<i>	Irony
<jk>	Just kidding
<>	No comment

Using Electronic Shorthand. Common expressions can be abbreviated in informal messages to save time; they're always capitalized. Here are several popular abbreviations.

Abbreviation	Expression
BRB	Be right back
BTW	By the way
CUL	See you later

Abbreviation	Expression
F2F	Face to face
FYA	For your amusement
FYI	For your information
HHOK	Ha ha only kidding
IMHO	In my humble opinion
OBTW	Oh, by the way
OIC	Oh, I see
ROFL	Rolling on the floor laughing
RTFM	Read the f-----g manual
SO	Significant other
TTFN	Ta-ta for now
TIA	Thanks in advance
TNX	Thanks
WRT	With respect to

Surviving Communication Triage.   The Subject line
is the first thing the recipient of your e-mail or news
posting views; as such it is often used for evaluating
whether your message will be read. Make your Subject
line as clear as possible to give the reader a good grasp
of what your message is about. After the Subject line, the
next most important part of your message is the first
screenful of information. Make your point as quickly and
concisely as possible. Many people who regularly work
with electronic communications receive large volumes
of messages. To get through these messages, people usually scan them as a form of reading triage. Messages that
are confusing or drone on without getting to the point
run the risk of not getting read.

Emphasizing Text.   Electronic communications is
pure text. Formatting text, such as italicizing words,
typically includes special control characters that can

wreak havoc when you use e-mail. Without formatting, some key statements can get lost in a sea of text. To indicate emphasis in your messages, place asterisks around a *word* or phrase you want to italicize and use underline characters before and after a _word_ or phrase you would like underlined. Both of these characters are recognized as emphasis indicators by most Internet users.

The Gordon Eubanks Rule. Rule number one in electronic communication: don't write a message that contains information you don't want to become public knowledge. Gordon Eubanks, president of Symantec, was indicted for conspiring to steal Borland trade secrets. The basis for the indictment was copies of e-mail messages sent to Eubanks found on a Borland employee's computer. Always keep in mind that any form of electronic communication is routinely saved in system backups, so they can be found. You don't know who may end up reading your communications.

Communications with an Attitude. At the risk of sounding like Mr. Rogers: be considerate of others' feelings. Don't send rude, harassing, or bigoted messages. Sarcasm in electronic communications is easily misunderstood. For example, the phrase "Yeah, right" can imply total agreement, but said in a sarcastic tone, it means the opposite. If you intend sarcasm, insert a sarcastic smiley into the message to denote that it is written with a cynical smile. Beyond netiquette, there is another good reason to control yourself. Most electronic communications can be traced, and systems on the Internet are liable for the activities of their users.

Keep Your Reader's Terminal in Mind. Keep the line length in your messages to less than 60 characters. You want messages to be capable of being displayed on any terminal. When a message is forwarded, it might end up on a screen that is indented by a tab character (usually 8 columns). Even though a sentence might wrap on your screen, it's not considered a line until you press **Enter.** Also, in some programs, such as the **vi** editor, if you forget to press **Enter** and exceed 256 characters, your screen will freeze up and you'll have to abort the message by pressing **Ctrl-C** twice. You shouldn't use the font features of your terminal, such as boldface and italics. These frequently send a string of control characters that create problems on terminals that are different from yours.

Don't SHOUT or use all lowercase.   Typing all upper-case letters is known as SHOUTING. Use mixed upper-case and lowercase as you would in any writing. In addition to being mistaken for shouting, a message writ-ten in uppercase letters is more difficult to read. Like-wise, using all lowercase in a message is annoying because it is hard to determine where sentences begin and end.

Don't Get Burned by Flaming.   The quick response features of electronic communications can easily cause a flare-up of angry exchanges. Ranting and raving via electronic communication is referred to as *flaming*. This kind of electronic verbal warfare goes on frequently. When in doubt about your emotions, let yourself cool down before responding to an offending message.

   Flaming isn't always a fighting match; just as some shock-jocks like to heat up their radio talk shows, the Internet is filled with users who love to spice things up. A lot of controversial topics and stances are taken with the user's tongue firmly in his or her cheek. The Internet is populated with frustrated comedians whose favorite pastime is flaming. If you think that a message is totally outrageous, it might be a joke waiting for you to add the punch line. A common convention to identify that you are knowingly venting your anger is to type

FLAME ON:

Message

FLAME OFF:

Check Twice, Think Twice.   Like slipping a letter through the mail slot in a post office box, once you press **Enter** to send your communications, you're committed. Read your messages twice before you send them and check to make sure you won't regret tomorrow what you've sent today.

   FYI: We lied about the quiz.

Chapter 2

COMMUNICATING VIA ELECTRONIC MAIL

Electronic mail is the number-one use of the Internet. Sending e-mail on the Internet is similar to sending mail through the post office, except it gets there almost instantaneously. Millions of people have mailboxes connected to the Internet highway. The Internet mail system extends well beyond the Internet itself to include virtually every commercial network, including CompuServe, America Online, Delphi, and MCI Mail. This chapter delivers hands-on instructions for communicating via e-mail using the friendly, menu-based e-mail program **pine**. The **pine** program is widely available on the Internet and offered as a mail program option by most service providers.

> **FYI:** If you don't have the **pine** program on your system, don't worry. We explain how to use the old standby UNIX mail programs **mail** and **mailx** in Chapter 7.

E-MAILING WITH PINE

The **pine** program acts as your local post office. It routes your message via the Internet to the recipient's mailbox and handles your incoming messages. Your user name and Internet address serve as the unique address for your e-mail. When someone sends you mail, it is delivered to

your incoming mailbox, usually a special file named
inbox, which is referred to as a *folder*.

If you're using an access provider and you don't have
access to **pine**, ask the provider to install it for you. We
guarantee you'll be glad if it's installed. The **pine** program was developed by the University of Washington as
an easier-to-use alternative to the UNIX **mail** and **mailx**
programs. It includes all the features you need to send,
read, and manage your e-mail, and you don't have to
remember a lot of commands the way you do with **mail**
and **mailx**.

> **FYI:** If you already have access to e-mail, chances are you
> can send e-mail to and receive mail from other users on the
> Internet without using the **pine** program. The one common
> element of all e-mail programs is that, to send e-mail to
> someone on the Internet, you use his or her e-mail address
> (*username@ Internet-address*). If you have a dedicated con-
> nection using a PC or Mac, numerous shareware and com-
> mercial mail programs are available.

GETTING STARTED WITH PINE

If you have any mail messages, a message appears after
you login informing you that you have mail. To start the
pine program, at the system prompt type **pine**. The first
time you start **pine**, it creates folders for storing messages and asks if you want create a folder named for the
current month for your sent messages. If you choose yes,
a folder, such as **sent-mail-nov-1993,** is created. Every
month **pine** will prompt you to create a new folder for
your sent messages. If you choose no, pine uses the
default **sent-mail** folder. When you start **pine**, you're
again told you have new mail. The Main Menu screen
appears, which is the starting point for working with any
part of the **pine** program.

Pressing the corresponding character to the right of the menu option displays a new screen for working with that option. **Pine** is not case sensitive. For example, pressing **C** or **c** displays the Compose Message screen for composing and sending your e-mail. At the bottom of any screen are commands for working in that screen. For example, in the Main Menu screen (shown in Figure 2-1), the commands for accessing the different features of **pine** are listed at the bottom of the screen. The letter or keystroke combination you press to execute the command is highlighted. When you see a command, such as ^T or ^O, the caret (^) character indicates you press the **Ctrl** key with the letter to execute the command.

The default choice in many **pine** prompts is displayed in brackets [ ], which means pressing **Enter** executes the choice. For example, pressing **Enter** in response to the following prompt tells **pine** not to cancel the message.

```
Cancelling will abandon your mail message. Cancel? [n]:
```

FYI: The **pine** program has a hidden configuration file, **.pinerc**, that you can edit with a text editor. See Chapter 7 for more information on hidden files and working with text editors.

Getting Help in pine

The **pine** program includes an extensive online help system that is *context sensitive*. Context sensitive means the help information that appears when the help command is entered is related to where the cursor is located

FIGURE 2.1
The Main Menu
screen

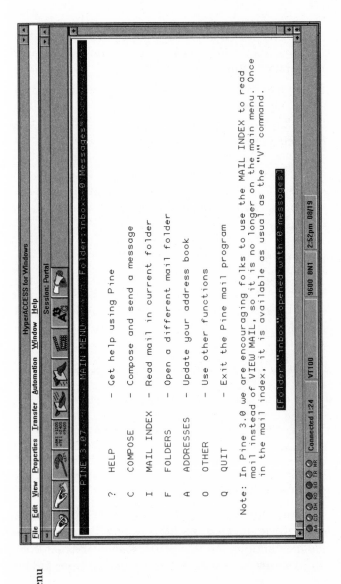

on the current screen. Depending on the where you're located in the **pine** program, you can access help either by pressing a question mark (**?**) or by pressing **Ctrl-G**. The help command is always displayed in the **pine** command menus at the bottom of each screen. The following are the most common commands for working in a help screen.

Command	Action
E	Exits the help system
L	Prints the help information to your local printer
- (hyphen)	Displays the previous page of help information
Spacebar	Displays the next page of help information
W	Searches for a text string in the current help information

COMPOSING AND SENDING E-MAIL

Now comes the time to share your exciting wit with other users by firing off an e-mail message. To begin composing a message, first press **C** to choose the Com– pose option from the Main Menu. The Compose Mes- sage screen appears (Figure 2-2), which includes the full range of tools you need to write, edit, and send your e-mail. Each message has two components: a header and a body. The message header includes the destination address, the subject of the message, and optional carbon copy information. The body of the message contains the text of your correspondence.

> **FYI:** Before you start sending e-mail messages, see Chap- ter 1 for netiquette guidelines for electronic communications and tips for writing effective e-mail.

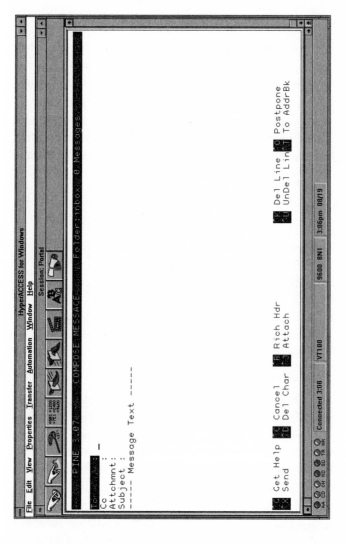

FIGURE 2.2

The Compose Message screen

Spicing Up Your John Hancock with a Signature File

When you compose a message, **pine** automatically searches for and includes in your outgoing message the contents of the **.signature** file in your home directory. A **.signature** file is a text file, usually about four lines in length, that contains additional information about you. Signature files typically contain your full name, postal address, fax number, other e-mail addresses, and so on. Many people like to include a quote. You must use a text editor, such as **vi** or **pico** (see Chapter 7), to create a **.signature** file. The following is a sample signature.

```
-------------------------------------------------
Butt-Head             |
butt-head@netcom.com  |
(415) 967-0559 voice  |   "Huh-huh, Huh-huh."
(415) 967-8283 fax    |
-------------------------------------------------
```

Navigating and Editing Messages

The **pine** program includes easy-to-use commands for navigating and editing text in the Compose Message screen. Many of these commands are listed in the menu at the bottom of the Compose Message screen. The following are the navigation commands for moving the cursor within the Compose Message screen.

Command	Moves Cursor
Right Arrow, Ctrl-F	One space to the right
Left Arrow, Ctrl-B	One space to the left
Up Arrow, Ctrl-P	One line up
Down Arrow, Ctrl-N	One line down
Ctrl-A	To the beginning of a line
Ctrl-E	To the end of a line

Command	Moves Cursor
Ctrl-@	To next word
Ctrl-Y	To the previous page
Ctrl-V	To the next page

The following are editing commands for working with text in the Compose Message screen.

Command	Action
Ctrl-K	Deletes the current line
Ctrl-U	Undeletes the last deleted line
Ctrl-D	Deletes the current character
Ctrl-H	Deletes the previous character
Backspace	Deletes character to the left of the cursor

Addressing Your Message

The To: and Subject: fields at the top of the Compose Message screen are the key fields in your message header. The To: field is the address of the person you want to send your message to, much like the address on a letter. You can send a message to more than one person by separating each e-mail address by a comma. For example,

```
butt-head@netcom.com, beavis@shell.portal.com
```

The Subject: field is for a brief description of your message. Remember, the Subject field is the line that most e-mail programs display for incoming messages. Make it as descriptive yet concise as possible. For example, entering the subject line

Subject: Looking for AC/DC tickets

is a lot more informative than

Subject: AC/DC Rocks

> **FYI:** The **pine** program includes a handy, time-saving address book that lets you keep track of your e-mail addresses and automatically inserts them into the To: field. See Keeping Your Little Black Book of E-mail Addresses later in this chapter for details.

Cc, Bcc, and Fcc.   The Cc: (carbon copy) field lets you send a carbon copy of your message to other people. A carbon copy is simply a copy of the message. You enter the e-mail address into the Cc: field in the same way you do for the To: field.

Pressing **Ctrl-R** in a header field displays additional mail header fields that include the Bcc: and Fcc: fields. The Bcc: (Blind carbon copy) field lets you send carbon copies of your message to other people without the person receiving the original message knowing you sent a carbon copy. You enter the address in the same way as for the To: and Cc: fields. The Fcc: (File carbon copy) field specifies the folder in which you want to store the message after you send it. The default folder **sent-mail** initially appears in the field. For now, don't worry about this field, because you can always move messages to folders later. Pressing **Ctrl-R** again shrinks the mail header to the basic set of fields.

Addressing E-mail for Other Networks.   Connection points between e-mail networks are computers called *gateways* because they act as translators that can communicate with other types of networks. To send mail through a gateway, you need to give an e-mail address that contains information about how to get to the

gateway and information about how to deliver the mail
on the other network. The easiest way to get the e-mail
address of someone is to ask for it from the recipient. If
you don't know the person's e-mail address but know his
or her user name and account network, you can use the
following table to address e-mail sent via the Internet.

Network	Syntax and Example
America Online	*username*@aol.com **bob@aol.com**
Applelink	*username*@applink.apple.com **bob@applink.apple.com**
ATTMail	*username*@attmail.com **bob@attmail.com**
BITNET	*username@host.bitnet* OR *username%host@gateway* Use the address of a Bitnet-Internet gateway for the machine name side; for example, **cunyvm.cuny.edu.s.** The address **bob@uiuccvmd.bitnet** becomes **bob%uiuccvmd.bitnet@cunyvm.cuny.edu**
BIX	*username*@bix.com **bob@bix.com**
CompuServe	*userid*@compuserve.com Change the comma in the CompuServe user's user ID to a period. The user ID 74640,2405 becomes **74640.2405@compuserve.com**
Delphi	*username*@delphi.com **bob@delphi.com**

Network	Syntax and Example
FidoNet	FidoNet addresses consist of a first and last name, and a set of numbers indicating the node (1:2/3.4). Separate the first and last names with a period (.) and insert the node numbers in the address as shown in the following example: **bob.newhart@p4.f3.n2.z1.fid onet.org**
GEnie	*username*@genie.geis.com **bob@genie.geis.com**
MCI Mail	*userid*@mcimail.com **or** *username*@mcimail.com Eliminate the hyphen in the MCI Mail user's ID. The user ID 353-1435 becomes 3531435. **3531435@mcimail.com** OR **bob@mcimail.com**
SprintMail	/G=givename/S=surname/O=Organization/ADMD=Telemail/C=US/@sprint.com A less exact syntax is firstname.lastname@organization.sprint.com **/G=Bob/S=Newhart/O=CBS/ADMD=TELEMAIL/C=US/@sprint.com** OR **bob.newhart@cbs.sprint.com**
UUCP	*uunet!host!username* **or** *username*@*domainname* **uunet!bookware!bob** OR **bob@portal.com**

> **FYI:**   A document entitled *The Internet Mailing Guide* con-
> tains additional information on sending mail to other net-
> works. It's available via **ftp** at site: **ra.msstate.edu**, directory:
> **/pub/docs**, file: **internetwork-mail-guide**. See Chapter 5 for
> information on using the **ftp** program.

Composing Your Message

The Message Text area of the Compose Message screen
is where you compose the body of your message. The
pine program uses a built-in version of the **pico** text
editor. The **pico** editor, which stands for **pi**ne **co**mposer,
allows you to work on text a screenful at a time. It is also
available as a stand-alone text editor. See Chapter 7 for
more information on working with **pico**.

In **pico**, text automatically wraps as you type past the
end of a line, so you do not have to hit **Enter** after each
line. The **pico** editor defines a word as any combination
of characters separated from adjacent characters by a
space. Paragraphs are separated by one blank line. The
Ctrl-J command lets you justify text in the paragraph
the cursor is on. This is handy for formatting a paragraph
in which the lines appear very uneven.

Cancelling or Postponing a Message

You can exit the Compose Message screen either by
cancelling the current message or by postponing the
message to work on it at another time. To cancel the
message you're currently working on, press **Ctrl-C**,
which displays the prompt

```
Cancelling will abandon your mail message. Cancel? [n]:
```

Press **y** to cancel the message and return to the Main Menu.

To postpone the current message, press **Ctrl-O**. The
message is saved and you're returned to the Main Menu.

You'll be prompted each time you choose the Compose option from the Main Menu, with the following prompt

```
Continue postponed composition (answering "No"
won't erase it)? (y/n) [y]:
```

until you send or delete the message.

Press **y** or **Enter** to continue working on the postponed message or press **n** to save the message to work on at a later time. Only one message can be postponed at a time.

Keeping Your Spelling in Check

To help keep your e-mail spellbinding, check the spelling of a message using **pine**'s spell checker. To perform a spelling check of a message, move the cursor to the beginning of your message, then press **Ctrl-T**. The spell checker starts checking the spelling of your message. When it finds a word it doesn't recognize, the spell checker displays the prompt, Edit a replacement: followed by the misspelled word. You can then enter the correct spelling for the word or press **Enter** to leave the original spelling intact and continue spell checking.

> **CAUTION:** Don't rely exclusively on the spell checker to police your spelling; spell checkers are by no means foolproof. Use the spell checker only as a helpful supplementary tool.

Inserting and Attaching Files

Why rewrite text if it already exists? The **pine** program lets you easily insert the contents of a text file into your message. Inserting text files into your messages allows you to bring in text from other sources or create a message offline, then insert it in your message instead of creating the message online. Any inserted text appears with a greater than symbol (>) at the beginning of each line to indicate the text was inserted into the message.

Of course, you can edit out the greater than symbols if you want.

You can also attach a file to a mail message to send along all kinds of information. You can attach a file of any kind, including binary files such as program, graphic, and sound files. The **pine** program makes attaching files easy by automatically compressing and encoding the file so that you don't have to. When you attach a file to a message, the contents of the file won't actually show in your message. Here is how to insert or attach a file to a message.

1. If you want to insert a text file into a message, position the cursor where you want the text from the file to be inserted in your message, then press **Ctrl-R**. The prompt Insert file: appears. If you want to attach a file, move the cursor to the Attchmnt: field, then press **Ctrl-J**. The prompt File to attach: appears.

2. If you know the name of the file, type the name of the file you want to insert or attach. If the file isn't located in your home directory, be sure to include the path name. After you press **Enter**, the text file is either inserted in or attached to your message.

3. If you don't know where a file is located, press **Ctrl-T**. A listing of the files and directories in your home directory appears. To view files in a directory (dir), use the **Arrow** keys to move the highlight to the directory, then press **Enter**. A prompt appears asking if you want to enter the directory. Press **y** or **Enter** to enter it. To move back up to the parent directory, choose .. (parent dir). Move the highlight to the file you want and press **S** or **Enter**.

4. If you're attaching a file, you can enter any optional comments about the file at the prompt. The file path name, the file size, and any comments you enter appear in the Attchmt field.

Searching for the Word

You can search a message for certain words, which is helpful if you want to change some particular text in a large message. To search for a word in your message, press **Ctrl-O**, then press **Ctrl-W**. The Search: prompt appears. Enter the text you want to search for and **pine** searches for a match. If matching text exists, the cursor moves to the beginning of the first occurrence of the search text. Press **Enter** to continue searching for the next occurrence. Any time you want to cancel the search, press **Ctrl-C**.

Sending Your Message

After you compose your message, press **Ctrl-X** to send it on its way. The **pine** program displays the Send message? [y]: prompt. Press **y** or press **Enter** to send the message. The message is sent and a copy of it is stored in the default **mail-sent** folder.

If you enter an incorrect address, the message is returned to your mailbox. Just as an envelope sent through the postal service gets postmarked showing the route it took, the mail header includes information added to it to help you find out what route it took and why the message was returned. In most cases, the reason for returned mail is as simple as a mistyped user name or address. However, undeliverable mail can occur because computers or pieces of the network are unavailable.

RECEIVING MAIL

You send mail, you get mail. Your incoming mail is stored in the **inbox** folder. To read and manage your incoming mail in **pine**, press **I** to choose the Mail Index option from the Main Menu screen. This displays the Mail Index screen (Figure 2-3).

FIGURE 2.3

The Mail Index
Screen

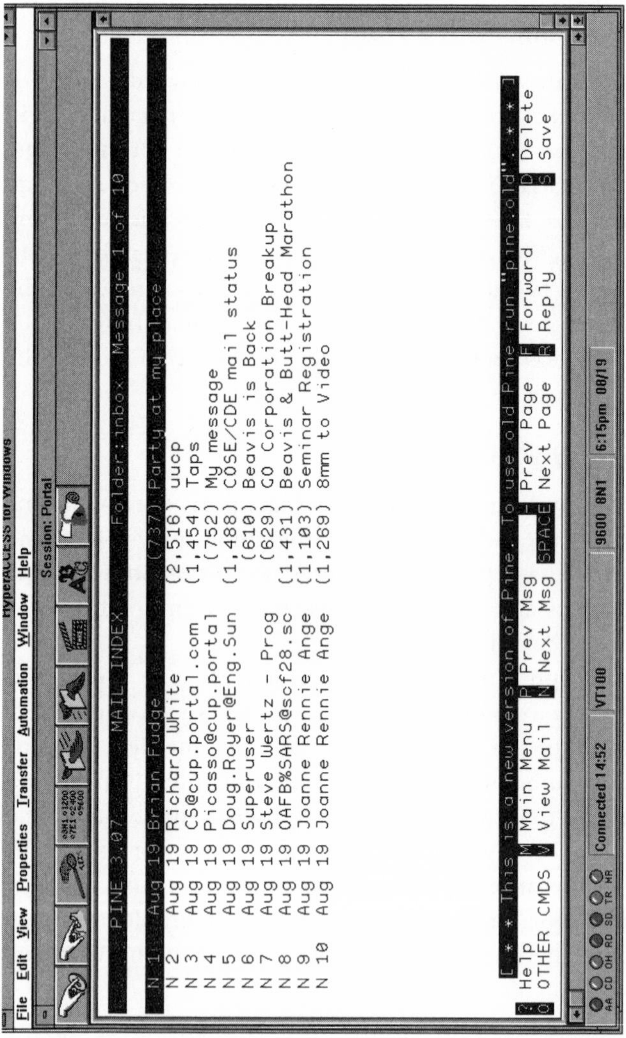

```
File  Edit  View  Properties  Transfer  Automation  Window  Help
                                                    hyperACCESS for Windows

                                                    Session: Portal

PINE 3.07          MAIL INDEX             Folder:inbox  Message 1 of 10

N  1  Aug 19  Brian Fudge        (  737) Party at my place
N  2  Aug 19  Richard White      (2,516) uucp
N  3  Aug 19  CS@cup.portal.com  (1,454) Taps
N  4  Aug 19  Picasso@cup.portal (  752) My message
N  5  Aug 19  Doug.Royer@Eng.Sun (1,488) COSE/CDE mail status
N  6  Aug 19  Superuser          (  610) Beavis is Back
N  7  Aug 19  Steve Wertz - Prog (  629) Go Corporation Breakup
N  8  Aug 19  OAFB%SARS@scf28.sc (1,431) Beavis & Butt-Head Marathon
N  9  Aug 19  Joanne Rennie Ange (1,103) Seminar Registration
N 10  Aug 19  Joanne Rennie Ange (1,269) 8mm to Video


[ * * This is a new version of Pine. To use old Pine run "pine.old". * * ]
? Help      M Main Menu    P Prev Msg    - Prev Page    F Forward    D Delete
O OTHER CMDS V View Mail   N Next Msg  SPACE Next Page   R Reply     S Save

     Connected 14:52   VT100   9600  8N1   6:15pm  08/19
```

Initially just the message header is displayed in the Mail Index screen, appearing as a single line. Message headers include information about the message and its current status. A listing of new message headers appears in the Mail Index screen, similar to this:

```
N 1 Nov 19 bob@sun.com      (293) Concert

N 2 Nov 19 claireho@aw.com (356) Tickets

N 3 Nov 20 phils@aw.com      (578) Schedule
```

The following describes each of the elements, from left to right, in the mail headers listing.

Column	Description
Status	The status of a message in the mailbox. N (new) indicates the message arrived since the last reading. A blank indicates the message has been read. D indicates the message is marked for deletion.
Number	Messages in a folder are numbered, from one through the number of messages in the folder. If you're viewing incoming messages, the numbers reflect the order in which the messages were received.
Date Sent	The date the message was sent. By default, messages are ordered chronologically by arrival time.
Sender	Address of the person who sent you the message.

Column	Description
Size	Number of characters in the message.
Subject	Subject of the message.

Sorting Your Mail

The default order of messages listed in a folder are based on date (and time if the message has the same date). You can sort messages in your Mail Index screen according to other criteria by pressing **Z**, which displays the prompt

```
Sort by Subject, [Arrival], From, Date, siZe,
Reverse (type S[A]FDZ or R):
```

Press the letter that corresponds to the sort you want to perform. The following describes each sort option.

Command	Sorts By
Subject	Subject lines of messages alphabetically
Arrival	Time of message's arrival, with the most recent first
From	Name of user names sending messages
Date	Date of messages with most recent first
siZe	Size of the message
Reverse	Oldest messages first (reverse of the default order)

Reading Your Mail

To read a message, move the highlight to the message you want to read using the **Down Arrow** or **Up Arrow** key, then press **V** or **Enter**. The message appears in the view mode. The following are commands for navigating the mail header list or messages in the view mode.

Command	Action
- (hyphen)	Moves to the previous page of mail headers or the previous page in a message
Spacebar	Moves to the next page of mail headers or the next page in a message
n	Displays the next message
p	Displays the previous message

You can jump to any message by using its message number. To jump to another message, press **O**, then **J**. A prompt appears asking you to enter the message number. When you enter the message number, the highlight moves to the message header or the message is displayed if you're in the view mode. The **pine** program doesn't automatically move your messages out of your **inbox** folder after you read them and quit the program. Moving messages between folders is explained later in this chapter.

> **TIP:** You can exit the **pine** program directly from the Mail Index screen by pressing **Q**.

Replying to Your Mail

You can reply to a message right from the Mail Index screen while your thoughts are still fresh. To reply to a message, highlight the mail header or display the message, then press **R**. The **pine** program displays the prompt

`Include the original message in Reply? (y/n) [n]:`

If you want to insert the original message, press **y**. A new message appears in the Compose Message screen with the address of the recipient in the `To:` field, and `RE:` followed by the original message's subject in the `Subject:` field. A line in the beginning of the message text gives the date of the message and the user name of the person you're replying to. The text from the inserted message is noted by the greater than symbol (>) inserted at the beginning of each line. You can proceed to edit the inserted text and compose your reply in the same way you compose a new message. After finishing your reply, press **Ctrl-X** to send it.

Forwarding a Message

Forwarding a message is like forwarding a letter: you add a new address to the message and send it off. It's a quick way to show someone a message you've received. To forward a message, highlight the message header or display the message you want to forward, then press **F**. A new message is created in the Compose Message screen containing the message you want to forward. Enter the e-mail address you want it forwarded to. You can add text to the message as you would for any message. Press **Ctrl-X** to send the message; it's then forwarded to the address you specify. When you send a forwarded message, (fwd) is appended to the Subject line. To help identify the forwarded message, the line

```
--------Forwarded message--------
```

appears directly above the message

Deleting and Undeleting Messages

E-mail has a way of piling up. To keep from cluttering up your mailbox, periodically chuck the mail messages you don't want. Keeping your messages to a minimum can also save you money if your service provider charges you for disk space (many do). In the Mail Index screen, you delete a message by highlighting the message and pressing **D**. Messages you specify for deletion are marked with a D to the left of the message header, but the message is not immediately deleted. If you have a change of heart, you can undelete a message by high-lighting the message and pressing **O**, then pressing **U**. Press **O** to return to the default Mail Index menu. The deletion mark is removed.

When you quit the **pine** program, you're prompted to confirm the deletion of the messages. Pressing **y** or **Enter** deletes from the **inbox** folder any messages marked for deletion. Pressing **n** keeps the messages in your inbox folder. If you want to delete immediately, all messages marked with a D, press **O**, then press **X**. The **pine** program prompts you to confirm the deletion, which you do by pressing **y** or **Enter** to delete the messages. Press **O** to return to the default Mail Index menu.

> **CAUTION:**   Once you delete a message and quit **pine**, the message is gone forever.

Saving a Message to a File

Saving a message as a text file allows you to work with it in a text editor. If you're using a service provider, you can download it to your computer to work on it. To save a message to a file highlight the message and press **O**, then press **E**. A prompt appears asking you to enter the file name you want to save the message under. If you want to save the file in a different directory other than your home directory, type the path name. The message is saved as a file and also remains as a message in the Mail Index listing. Press **O** to return to the default Mail Index menu.

Saving a Message to Another Folder

To manage your messages better, you can create and store messages in folders. You can even create a folder at the same time you save the message. Folders are special files for storing mail messages. Working with folders is explained in greater detail a little later in this chapter. To

save a message in an existing folder or save a message and
create a new folder at the same time, do the following:

1. Choose the message header or display the message
   you want to store in the Mail Index screen.
2. Press **S**. A prompt appears asking you to enter the
   name of the folder.
3. If you want to save the message to an existing folder
   and know the name of the folder, enter it. If you don't
   know the name of the folder, press **Ctrl-T**. A listing of
   all your folders appears. When you choose the folder,
   the message is saved to the folder and the message is
   marked for deletion in the Mail Index listing.
4. To save the message to a folder that doesn't exist, enter
   the new folder name. The **pine** program asks if you
   want to create it. Press **y** or **Enter** to create the folder.
   The message is saved to the new folder and the message
   is marked for deletion in the Mail Index listing.

Searching for the Word

You can search for a word in a message header listing or in
a message by first pressing **O**, then pressing **W**, which
displays a prompt asking you to enter the text you want to
search for. When you enter your text, **pine** searches for a
match in the mail header list or the current message depending on what is displayed. If matching text exists, the cursor
moves to the beginning of the first occurrence of the search
text. Press **Enter** to continue searching for the next occurrence. You can cancel a search at any time by pressing
Ctrl-C.

Printing a Message

There are times when you need a hard copy of a message
to keep on file or pass around. You can print a message
on your local printer by pressing **O**, then **L**. A prompt
appears asking you to confirm printing. Press **y** or **Enter**

to print the message. The message is printed at your local printer. This printing feature is particularly useful if you're using a service provider and want a hard copy of the message at your local computer. If you're printing a long message, it can take a few minutes because the text and formatting codes are downloaded to your printer.

> **Caution:** This may not work with all printers and will depend on the communications software you're using.

Working with Attachments

The **pine** program is a terrific time saver when it comes to file attachments. When you receive an attached file, **pine** automatically uncompresses and decodes it. A message that includes an attached file or multiple files informs you in the header that the message has attachments. The mail message and each attachment has its own number. The **pine** program gives you the option of viewing a text file on your screen. To view or save an attached file, do the following:

1. In the Mail Index screen, highlight the message and press **Enter** to display the mail message. Information appears at the top of the message telling you if the attached file can be displayed.

2. Press **A**. A prompt appears asking you to enter the file attachment number. In most cases, any message text that the sender has added is positioned as part 1.

3. Enter the number of the file attachment you want. A prompt appears asking if you want to save or view the attachment.

4. If the attachment is a text file and you want to view it, press **V**. If you want to save the attachment as a file, press **S**. A prompt appears requesting you to enter the file name you want for the attachment. If you want to store an attached file in any directory other than your home directory, be sure to include the path name.

Downloading a File to Your Computer. If you're using a service provider to connect to the Internet and want the file on your computer, you will need to download the file from your account to your local computer. In most cases, the **sx** command is used to send a single file using the XModem protocol. The **sz** command sends one or more files using the ZModem protocol. ZModem is faster and can download multiple files. If your communications software supports the ZModem protocol, use it. To download a message that has been saved as a file named **letter.txt** using the ZModem protocol to your local computer, in your home directory enter **sz letter.txt** and issue the command from your local communications software to receive the file in the same protocol you're using to send the file.

KEEPING YOUR LITTLE BLACK BOOK OF E-MAIL ADDRESSES

The **pine** program's address book acts as a kind of speed dial for your electronic mail. Entering e-mail addresses in the address book makes them available for quick insertion into the To:, Cc:, and Bcc: fields of your messages. No more filling out these fields manually each time you want to send a message. To open the address book, choose the Addresses option from the Main Menu by pressing **A**. Figure 2-4 contains a sample address book screen with address entries.

The first column in an address entry is the *nickname,* also referred to as an *alias*. The nickname references the address book entry and inserts the corresponding e-mail address or addresses into the To:, Cc:, and Bcc: fields. The second column is descriptive information about the address book entry. The third column is the e-mail address column. Any address book entry that includes more than one e-mail address, has the DISTRIBUTION LIST header above the e-mail addresses.

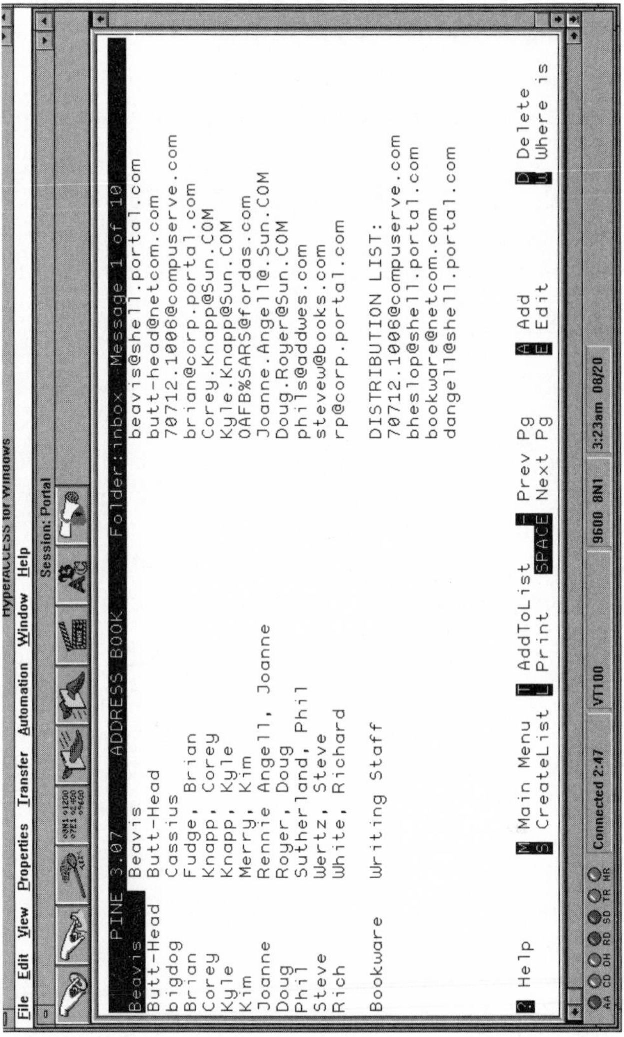
HyperACCESS for Windows
File Edit View Properties Transfer Automation Window Help
Session: Portal
PINE 3.07 ADDRESS BOOK Folder: inbox Message 1 of 10
Beavis Beavis beavis@shell.portal.com
Butt-Head Butt-Head butt-head@netcom.com
bigdog Cassius 70712.1006@compuserve.com
Brian Fudge, Brian brian@corp.portal.com
Corey Knapp, Corey Corey.Knapp@Sun.COM
Kyle Knapp, Kyle Kyle.Knapp@Sun.COM
Kim Merry, Kim 0AFB%SARS@fordas.com
Joanne Rennie Angell, Joanne Joanne.Angell@.Sun.COM
Doug Royer, Doug Doug.Royer@Sun.COM
Phil Sutherland, Phil phils@addwes.com
Steve Wertz, Steve stevew@books.com
Rich White, Richard rp@corp.portal.com
Bookware Writing Staff DISTRIBUTION LIST:
70712.1006@compuserve.com
bheslop@shell.portal.com
bookware@netcom.com
dangell@shell.portal.com
? Help M Main Menu T AddToList - Prev Pg A Add D Delete
S CreateList L Print SPACE Next Pg E Edit W Where is
Connected 2:47 VT100 9600 8N1 3:23am 08/20

FIGURE 2.4
The Address Book screen with entries

Creating an Address Book Entry

You can create an address book entry for a single person or for a group of people under a single nickname. For example, if you regularly send e-mail to a group, you can create an address book entry for all the users in that group. Entries are listed in two groups: single entries first, group entries second. Entries within these categories are listed alphabetically by nickname.

To add a new individual address, press **A**. At the prompt, `New full name (last, first):` type the person's full name, last name, then first name. This appears in the description column of the address entry. The **pine** program then prompts you for a nickname. Enter a short, one-word nickname that is easy to remember. This name is the name you enter in the `To:` header field to indicate the corresponding e-mail addresses. After you enter the nickname, **pine** prompts you for the e-mail address. Enter the e-mail address.

To create an address book entry for a group of people:
1. Press **S** in the Address Book screen. A prompt asks you to enter a description (long name) of your entry.
2. Enter a descriptive name for your address book entry. A prompt appears telling you to enter a short, one-word nickname that is easy to remember for your entry.
3. Enter a nickname. A prompt appears telling you to enter the first e-mail address.
4. Enter the first e-mail address. The same prompt appears for you to enter another e-mail address. After entering all your e-mail addresses, at the prompt press **Enter.**

Taking an Address from the Mail Index Screen

You can quickly add the e-mail address of the sender of any e-mail you've received into your address book directly from the Mail Index screen. Here is how to take an address from the Mail Index screen and add it to your address book.

1. In the Mail Index screen, move the highlight to the message header you want to add to your address book.
2. Press **O**. A menu of other **pine** commands appears.
3. Press **T**. A prompt appears telling you to enter a short, one-word nickname that is easy to remember for your entry.
4. Enter a nickname. A prompt appears with the full name of the person already entered, as it appears in the message header.
5. If the name is correct, press **Enter**. Otherwise enter the last name, a comma, a space, and the first name of the person for your address book entry. A prompt appears for an e-mail address with the e-mail address already entered.
6. Press **Enter**. The entry is added to your address book.

Managing Your Address Book Entries

Your e-mail addresses change, new users are added, old ones are deleted. The address book provides tools for managing your entries. It lets you delete an entire entry or a specific e-mail address in a DISTRIBUTION LIST. It also lets you add new users to an existing group, edit any part of an entry, print a list of your address book entries, and search your address book for specific information. Here are the commands for managing your address book entries.

Command	Description
D	Deletes an entire address book entry or deletes the highlighted e-mail address in a DISTRIBUTION LIST

Command	Description
E	Allows you to edit an item in the address book
T	Lets you add an e-mail address to a DISTRIBUTION LIST
L	Prints a copy of your address book at your local printer
W	Searches your address book for the text you specify

MANAGING YOUR MAIL FOLDERS

Every message is stored in a folder in your mail directory, which on a UNIX system is usually **/usr/spool /mail/*username***. The **pine** program initially creates three default folders, which are:

Folder	Description
inbox	Stores incoming messages. After messages are read, they are moved to the saved-messages folder.
saved-messages	Stores your messages after they have been read.
sent-mail	Stores messages you have sent. If you specify that **pine** create a new **sent-mail** folder for each month, the folder has a name like **sent-mail-nov-1993**.

The **pine** program uses these three folders to store your messages. You can create your own folders for storing messages you've already read or sent. Messages can be moved from one folder to another folder from the Mail Index screen. By default, the Mail Index screen displays messages in your **inbox** folder, but you can display the messages from any folder.

Press **F** to choose the `Folders` option from the Main Menu screen. This accesses the Folder Maintenance screen, which lists all your folders. Once you open a folder, the Mail Index screen is activated. If your listing of folders is greater than a single screenful, use the Spacebar to move to the next page or the **-** (hyphen) key to move to the previous page.

The last folder that you open becomes the default folder for the session. For example, if you open a folder with no messages and display the Mail Index screen, no mail headers will appear. To return to your original default mail folder, return to the Folder Maintenance menu and open the **inbox** folder.

The following commands let you work with your folders in the Folder Maintenance screen.

Command	Description
A	Adds a new empty folder. You can also create a folder when you save a message from the Mail Index screen.
D	Deletes a folder and all the messages in it. Once you confirm the deletion of a folder it cannot be recovered. If you delete the folder that is currently open, the folder is closed, then deleted, and the **inbox** folder is opened.
R	Renames a folder. The **pine** program prompts you for the new name of the folder.
O	Opens the highlighted folder so the messages in it can be worked on. Any previously opened folder is automatically closed.

Command	Description
G	Goes to a specific folder and opens it. After you press **G**, **pine** prompts you to specify the folder. This is useful for accessing any folders created in another directory.
W	Searches for a specific folder. A prompt appears asking you to enter the folder name If the folder has a unique name, you can enter the first few characters instead of the complete name.
L	Prints a list of all your folders.

> **CAUTION:** Don't edit a folder with a text editor. Editing a folder with a text editor can damage the folder, making it impossible for **pine** to read it.

Moving Messages between Folders

You manage the messages in any folder the same way you work with messages in your **inbox** folder. To move a message between folders, select the message, then press **S**. A prompt appears asking you to enter the folder name. If you don't know the folder name, press **Ctrl-T** to display your folders in the Folder Maintenance screen, then select the folder. You can also create a new folder by simply typing in the name you want for the folder. The **pine** program tells you there is no folder by that name and asks if you want to create it. Press **y** or **Enter** to create and save the message. The message in the original folder is marked for deletion.

WORKING WITH PINE UTILITIES

The Other option in the Main Menu screen provides access to a collection of **pine** utilities. To display the menu of utilities, press **O**.

Menu Option (Press)	Description
HELP (?)	Displays help on the other options in this menu.
NEWS (N)	Displays release notes for the current version of **pine** as well as a revision history of the **pine** program.
LOCK (K)	Lets you lock your keyboard to prevent someone gaining access to your mail while **pine** is active and you're not at your computer.
MAIN MENU (M)	Returns you to the Main Menu screen.
PASSWORD (P)	Lets you change your login password.
PRINTER (L)	Specifies the printer to print output to.
DISK (D)	Displays the amount of disk space being used for mail folders. The display includes the number of mail folders, space used by the mail folders, the free space for mail on the disk drive, and the path name of your mail directory.

QUITTING PINE

After you start the **pine** program, a working buffer is created in memory in which tasks you perform within **pine**, such as moving and deleting messages, are temporarily stored. These changes are stored to disk only when you quit **pine**. How you quit **pine** depends on where you are in the **pine** program. For all the submenu screens, except Compose Message, pressing **M** returns you to the Main Menu. To exit the Compose Message screen, press **Ctrl-C** to cancel your message and return to the Main Menu, or press **Ctrl-O** to postpone a message (save it to work on at another time) and return to the Main Menu. You can also exit the **pine** program directly from the Mail Index screen by pressing **Q**.

Once you are in the Main Menu, press **q** to quit the **pine** program. If you have deleted any messages during the current session, **pine** displays the following message to confirm the deletion of messages.

```
Expunge the deleted messages from "inbox"? <y/n> [y]:
```

Press **y** or **Enter** to delete the messages and quit **pine**.

Chapter 3

TURNING ON NETWORK NEWS

Network news is a massive, distributed bulletin board system with thousands of ongoing discussions covering every topic imaginable. People who subscribe to newsgroups communicate using a messaging system that is similar to e-mail. News articles range in tone from the seriousness of the "Mac-Neil/Lehrer NewsHour" to the gossipy outrageousness of the *National Enquirer*. No matter what your interest, the Internet has news for you. This chapter explains how to use the friendly **tin** news reader to participate actively in newsgroups.

WHAT IS NETWORK NEWS?

Network news is delivered via the UNIX-based network known as USENET. USENET is not actually part of the Internet, but it is widely available because so many systems on the Internet are running UNIX. Each USENET site collects and sends information to other sites. These sites in turn add their items then forward them. In this way articles are propagated throughout the network usually within 24 hours. USENET discussions are called *newsgroups*. Each newsgroup refers to a particular topic and contains *articles* related to that topic that are *posted* (sent) by individuals. Newsgroups can also include files that can be downloaded. To work with network news, you use a news reader program. Most news reader programs let you control which newsgroups you subscribe to. You can then read articles, respond to articles, post articles, and transfer files.

> **FYI:** The newsgroup **news.announce.newuser** provides helpful information for new users. An in-depth explanation of the USENET news system is available via **ftp** at site: **pit-manager.mit.edu,** directory: **pub/usenet/news.answers/news-answers/what-is -usenet,** file: **part 1.** See Chapter 5 for information on how to work with the **ftp** program.

DIGESTING NEWSGROUPS

Depending on your site, you can have access to thousands of newsgroups. These newsgroups are dynamic; they are continually being created or eliminated. At first glance, there may not appear to be an order to this news madness, but there is. Newsgroups are structured hierarchically, with the main topic appearing in the first part of the name, followed by subtopics. The name of each topic is separated from its subtopics by periods. For example, the newsgroup **comp.unix.questions** is a computer newsgroup concentrating on questions about UNIX. Many newsgroups are moderated; that is, a moderator decides whether or not a submission has relevance to the topic. To help you get your bearings, the following table includes popular main newsgroup topics and fifty of the most popular newsgroups.

Newsgroup Topic	Newsgroups
alt Alternative newsgroups that vary in subject matter ranging from political activism to sex stories	alt.activism alt.bbs alt.binaries.pictures.misc alt.binaries.pictures.erotica alt.cyberpunk alt.usage.english alt.pictures alt.pictures.binaries alt.sex alt.sources
comp Computer science and related topics, including software sources, and information on hardware and software systems	comp.ai comp.sys.ibm.pc comp.binaries. ibm.pc comp.graphics comp.lang.c comp.misc comp.os.msdos comp.sys.mac. hardware comp.unix.questions comp.unix.wizards comp.windows.x
misc Topics that don't fit into other categories or that fit into several categories	misc.taxes misc.wanted misc.forsale misc.jobs.offered misc.jobs.resumes misc.jobs.contract

Newsgroup Topic	Newsgroups
news Information on network news and USENET	news.announce.important news.announce.newusers news.newusers. questions news.groups news.lists
rec Hobbies, recreational activities, and the arts	rec.arts.books rec.arts.movies rec.arts.movies.reviews rec.games.mud.announce rec.mag rec.humor
sci Scientific research and applying computer science	sci.astro sci.space sci.med sci.physics sci.psychology
soc Social issues — the meaning of social can range from politically relevant to socializing, or anything in between	soc.politics soc.cultur.japan soc.feminism soc.roots

Newsgroup Topic	Newsgroups
talk	talk.bizarre
A forum for debate on controversial topics	talk.rumors
	talk.politics.mideast
	talk.religion.misc

Some newsgroups contain information for a particular region or organization. The following prefixes are examples of regional or organizational newsgroups.

Newsgroup Topic	Description
ca	California
ba	San Francisco Bay area
tx	Texas
su	Stanford University
de	Germany
att	AT&T
well	The WELL conferencing system

I READ THE NEWS WITH TIN TODAY, OH BOY

You need a TV to view the nightly news. Likewise, you need a news reader program to read newsgroups. The **tin** program represents a new generation of news reader programs that dramatically simplify working with network news. What makes **tin** better than most news readers is that it provides an easy-to-use menu system that consolidates reading, downloading, and posting functions into one program. There are three main levels of operation in the **tin** program that correspond to the hierarchy of network news.

- The newsgroup level lets you manage your newsgroups.
- The thread level lists all the discussions within a news-group. In USENET lingo, discussions are called *threads*, which refers to USENET's system of linking messages together to form discussions. Each thread starts with the original base article that begins the discussion, which is then expanded upon by follow-up articles.
- The article level is where you read or post messages associated with the thread topic. Articles are the heart and soul of network news. They're the actual exchanges between people that make up a thread.

> **FYI:** If you're using an IBM PC or Mac with a dedicated Internet connection, there are news reader programs that can be used instead of **tin**. For IBM PCs, the **Trumpet** news reader comes in both DOS and Windows versions. For the Mac, **NewsWatcher** and **HyperNews** are two news readers. For a listing and comparison of news reader programs with information on where to get the programs, ftp (see Chapter 5) to site: **pit-manager.mit.edu**, directory: **pub/usenet/news.answers/usenet-software**, file: **part1**.

GETTING STARTED WITH tin

To start the **tin** program, at the system prompt, enter **tin**. The **tin** program starts by displaying its current version number and begins reading several files on your system related to network news. Depending on the number of newsgroups available on your system, it can take **tin** several minutes to read these files. The first time you start **tin**, an introduction screen appears, prompting you to press any key to continue. After you press a key, the Group Selection screen (Figure 3-1) appears with a screenful of newsgroups.

> **TIP:** Not all terminals support highlighting. If the selected newsgroup doesn't appear with a highlight, press **l** to change the highlight to an arrow to identify your selections.

FIGURE 3.1

The Group
Selection screen

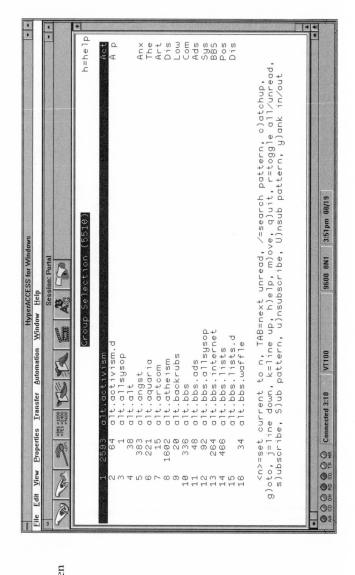

Many commands you work with in the different levels of **tin** are similar; the most common commands are displayed at the bottom of each screen. Keep in mind that **tin** is case sensitive. When you execute a command, the **tin** program often displays a prompt with a default choice appearing in brackets or following the prompt. For example, the default choice in the following prompt is n (no).

```
Subscribe to new group alt.zima (y/n/q) [n]:
```

Pressing n or **Enter** executes the default choice.

Getting Help in tin

The **tin** program's online help system is limited. It merely displays a list of commands with brief descriptions for the level you're currently working in. To display the listing of **tin** commands for the current level, press **h**. Pressing **H** toggles the minihelp menu to appear or not appear at the bottom of the screen. Removing this menu allows you to display four more lines on your screen.

Quitting the tin Program

You can quit **tin** from any location by typing **q**, which brings you to the previous level of **tin** until you reach the Group Selection screen. At the Group Selection screen, entering **q** quits the **tin** program. You can also quit **tin** directly from any level by pressing **Q**. Any changes you've made during a session are automatically saved.

WORKING WITH NEWSGROUPS

At the newsgroup level, you manage what newsgroups you subscribe to or unsubscribe from, and remove or change locations of newsgroups. Depending on your service provider or site, your listing of newsgroups can be overwhelming at first glance. By default you are automatically subscribed to all the newsgroups listed in the Group Selection screen. This means that any new articles posted are added to the ones already in the newsgroup. It will take some time to browse through the newsgroups and decide which ones you want to unsubscribe from. Don't feel like you have to make these decisions the first time you use **tin**. You can streamline your list of newsgroups on an ongoing basis.

Navigating the Newsgroup Listing

Because you're likely to be dealing with a large listing of newsgroups, the **tin** program includes a number of commands for navigating the newsgroup listing. The following are commands for navigating newsgroups.

Command	Moves
Spacebar, Ctrl-D, Ctrl-F	Down one page at a time.
b, Ctrl-U, Ctrl-B	Up one page at a time.
$	To the end of the newsgroup list.
Up Arrow, k	Up one line.
Down Arrow, j	Down one line.
n	To newsgroup number *n*. For example to move to newsgroup number 2100, type **2100**. The prompt Select group> appears followed by the number you entered. Pressing **Enter** moves to the newsgroup.

Command	Moves
g *newsgroup*	To the newsgroup specified. For example entering **g alt.binaries.pictures**. moves you directly to the **alt.binaries.pictures** newsgroup. If you press **g** by itself, tin displays the prompt, Goto newsgroup []>. Enter the newsgroup name you want to go to. The default newsgroup that appears in the brackets is the last newsgroup that you moved to. If you want to move to the newsgroup in the brackets, press **Enter**.

Searching for a Newsgroup

You can search newsgroups for specific text in the newsgroup name. To search for text in a newsgroup name, press / (slash) to initiate a forward search through the newsgroups from the position of the cursor. Press **?** to initiate a backward search. For example, suppose you want to jump ahead to a newsgroup that discusses jokes. At the newsgroup level, enter /. The **tin** program displays the prompt, Search forwards []>. Enter **humor** at the prompt to move to the next newsgroup containing the word **humor**. If you want to search backward for humor, press **?**; **tin** displays the prompt, Search backwards [humor]>. Pressing **Enter** searches backward for the text **humor**.

> **TIP:** Moving the cursor to the beginning or the end of the newsgroup listing before executing the search command lets you search in one direction through the entire list. Press the number **1** to move to the beginning of the list or press **$** to move to the end of the list.

Cancel My Subscription!

The key to working with news is effectively managing the number of newsgroups you participate in. If you have access to a large number of newsgroups, you will want to boil down the number of active newsgroups by unsubscribing from the ones you're not interested in. The **tin** program stores information about the newsgroups you're subscribed to in the **.newsrc** file. When you unsubscribe to a newsgroup, it is removed from the **.newsrc** file. When you unsubscribe from a newsgroup, a u appears to the left of the newsgroup number, indicating its status is unsubscribed. The next time the **tin** program reads your news files, any newsgroup marked as unsubscribed is removed from the listing. Don't worry — if you change your mind, you can redisplay your unsubscribed newsgroups and resubscribe to any of them at any time.

You can unsubscribe from a single newsgroup at a time or you can specify a group of newsgroups to unsubscribe from. To unsubscribe from a single newsgroup, navigate to that newsgroup, then press **u**. A more powerful version of unsubscribe allows you to unsubscribe from multiple newsgroups, matching the text pattern you specify. To unsubscribe from multiple newsgroups, press **U**. The **tin** program responds with the prompt

```
Enter regex unsubscribe pattern>
```

The term *regex* refers to a regular expression that, in plain English, means letters, numbers, and any wild-card characters. Entering **alt.*** unsubscribes from all newsgroups beginning with **alt**. Entering **alt.binaries.*** unsubscribes from all newsgroups beginning with **alt.binaries**, and entering **alt.binaries.pictures*** unsubscribes from all newsgroups beginning with **alt.binaries.pictures**.

> **FYI:** You can unsubscribe from all the newsgroups at one
> time then selectively subscribe to newsgroups using a text
> editor to edit your **.newsrc** file. See the section Customizing
> **tin** later in this chapter.

Resubscribing to Newsgroups

Any newsgroup that has been unsubscribed from can be
resubscribed to. To display your unsubscribed newsgroups, press **y**. The **y** (yank) command yanks all your
unsubscribed newsgroups from the **.newsrc** file, which
is a hidden file that keeps track of newsgroups. All the
unsubscribed newsgroups appear in the newsgroup listing in alphabetical order and are identified by a u to the
left of their newsgroup number.

Subscribing to newsgroups is performed in a manner
similar to unsubscribing from newsgroups. To subscribe
to a single newsgroup, navigate to that newsgroup, then
press **s**. The u is removed and you're subscribed to the
newsgroup. You can subscribe to multiple newsgroups
matching a text pattern by using the **S** command. For
example, entering **S** displays the prompt

```
Enter regex subscribe pattern>
```

Entering **alt.*** at this prompt subscribes you to all newsgroups beginning with **alt**. Entering **alt.binaries.*** subscribes to all newsgroups beginning with **alt.binaries**,
and entering **alt.binaries.pictures*** subscribes to all
newsgroups beginning with **alt.binaries.pictures**.

No News Is Good News: Killing Newsgroups

You can kill (delete) a newsgroup, which is different
from unsubscribing from a newsgroup. When you kill
a newsgroup from **tin**, it removes the newsgroup name
from the **.newsrc** file. Killing a newsgroup means you
can't redisplay it by using the **y** (yank) command. The
tin program allows you to kill only one newsgroup at a

time. To kill a newsgroup, move to that newsgroup, then press **Ctrl-K**. A prompt appears asking you to confirm the deletion of the newsgroup. Pressing **y** or **Enter** removes the newsgroup name from the Group Selection screen.

> **TIP:** If you accidentally kill a newsgroup, press **Z** to undelete it. You can continue to undelete each newsgroup you killed in the current session by pressing **Z** for each newsgroup.

Changing Newsgroup Positions

By repositioning newsgroups to appear at the beginning of the newsgroups list you can save the time of navigating to newsgroups you frequently participate in. For example, to change newsgroup number 100 to newsgroup number 1, enter **100** to move to newsgroup 100 and press **m**. The following prompt appears

```
Position newsgroup_name in group list (1,2,.,$) [100]>
```

Enter **1** to move the newsgroup to the top of the list. A message informs you that **tin** is moving the newsgroup. The newsgroup is moved and it appears at its new location and the newsgroups are renumbered.

Subscribing to New Newsgroups

The first time you use the **tin** program it automatically subscribes you to all the currently available newsgroups. There are new newsgroups being created all the time. If new newsgroups were created since you last used **tin,** when you start **tin,** it presents each new newsgroup name and asks you if you want to subscribe to the newsgroup. The prompt looks like this:

```
Subscribe to new group alt.zima (y/n/q) [n]:
```

If you want to subscribe to the newsgroup and add it to your newsgroup listing, press **y**. If the newsgroup doesn't interest you, press **Enter** or **n**. The **tin** program displays the next newsgroup. Any time you want to quit subscribing to new newsgroups, press **q**. This suspends the listing of new newsgroups until the next time you start **tin**.

> **TIP:** To skip listing the new newsgroups and start working with **tin** immediately, enter **tin -q** at the system prompt. When you're ready, you can enter just **tin** (without **-q**) to consider the new newsgroups.

THREAD FUNDAMENTALS

Threads are a chain of related articles. These articles are posted in response to the initial base article that starts the thread. A thread can be as small as a base article with no responses or it can be as large as thousands of articles (responses). The thread level displays a listing of the subject information about the original article that started the discussion and the number of articles attached to the base article. Articles are listed in a thread in a simple linear manner based on the order they were posted to the thread. You can display any threads connected to a newsgroup by moving to the newsgroup you want, then pressing **Enter**. A screenful of threads appears (Figure 3-2). At the top of the screen is the newsgroup name followed by the number of threads and articles. For example, 56T means 56 threads, and 103A means 103 articles are connected to those 56 threads.

Navigating Threads

Many of the navigation commands for moving through the listing of threads are similar to those for moving through newsgroups. Here are the common navigation commands for moving through a thread listing.

FIGURE 3.2

A thread listing

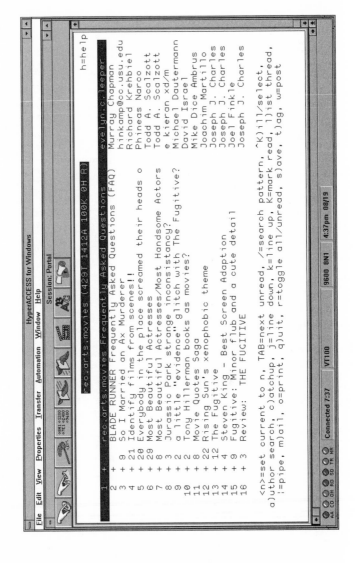

Command	Moves
Spacebar, Ctrl-D, Ctrl-F	Down one page at a time.
b, Ctrl-U, Ctrl-B	Up one page at a time.
$	To the end of the newsgroup list.
Up Arrow, k	Up one line.
Down Arrow, j	Down one line.
n	To thread number *n*. For example to move to thread number 35, type **35**. The prompt Select thread> appears followed by the number you entered. Pressing **Enter** moves to the thread.
q	To the Group Selection screen.

Killing Threads

You may want to subscribe to a newsgroup but eliminate specific threads in that newsgroup. To kill a thread, move to it, then press **Ctrl-K**. The **tin** program displays the Kill/Auto-select Article Menu screen. Press **Enter** until the cursor appears at the bottom of the screen. The following prompt appears

```
q)uit e)dit s)ave kill/hot description: s
```

Press **Enter** to complete the killing of the thread. A reference to the specific thread is added to a file named **kill** located in your **.tin** directory. The kill file keeps track of threads that you don't want displayed.

Marking Threads as Read and Unread

If you read any article in a thread by pressing **Enter** to open it, **tin** marks the article as read. This changes the number of articles listed before thread names in the thread listing screen. If you read all the articles in a thread, the thread is marked as read. This means that **tin** updates your **.newsrc** file, so the read articles or thread no longer shows up when you read news. You can mark a thread as unread even if you've read it, or mark a thread as read if you haven't read it. Here are commonly used commands for marking threads as read or unread, and commands for displaying read or unread threads.

Command	Effect
c	Marks as read all articles in a newsgroup; returns you to the newsgroup level
C	Marks as read all articles in the newsgroup; goes to the first article of the next unread thread
r	Toggles to show all articles or only unread articles
Z	Marks all articles as unread in the current thread
K	Marks all articles as read in the current thread

FYI: You can also mark threads as read or unread from the newsgroup level. Press **c** to mark all articles as read or press **z** to mark the entire newsgroup as unread.

ARTICLE FUNDAMENTALS

To display articles in a thread, navigate to the thread you want and press **Enter**. The **tin** program indexes the articles in the thread. The larger the number of articles in the thread, the longer it takes **tin** to index it. You can abort the indexing by pressing **q**. After **tin** finishes indexing the thread, it displays the first page of the base article (an example is shown in Figure 3.3). The base article is the article that started the thread. Each follow-up article added after the base article is referred to as a *response* in the **tin** program. The name of the thread appears at the top of the

FIGURE 3.3

An article
displayed in the
article level

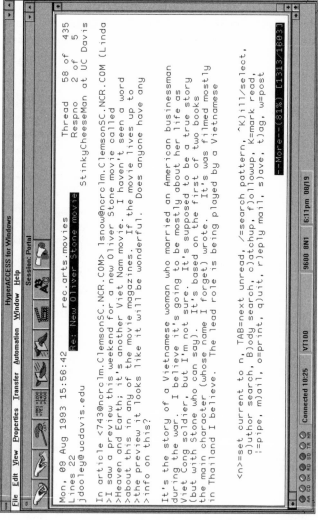

```
File  Edit  View  Properties  Transfer  Automation  Window  Help
                                          HyperACCESS for Windows
                                    Session: Portal

Mon, 09 Aug 1993 15:56:42      rec.arts.movies              Thread  58 of 435
Lines 22                     Re: New Oliver Stone movie       Respno   2 of   5
jdooley@ucdavis.edu                              StinkyCheeseMan at UC Davis

In article <743@ncrclm.ClemsonSC.NCR.COM> lsnow@ncrclm.ClemsonSC.NCR.COM (Linda
>I saw a preview this weekend for a new Oliver Stone movie called
>Heaven and Earth; it's another Viet Nam movie. I haven't seen a word
>about this in any of the movie magazines. If the movie lives up to
>the preview it looks like it will be wonderful. Does anyone have any
>info on this?

It's the story of a Vietnamese woman who married an American businessman
during the war.  I believe it's going to be mostly about her life as
Viet Cong soldier, but I'm not sure. It's supposed to be a true story
(but with Stone who can say). It's based on the first of two books
the main character (whose name I forget) wrote.  It's was filmed mostly
in Thailand I believe.  The lead role is being played by a Vietnamese

<n>=set current to n, TAB=next unread, /=search pattern, ^K)ill/select,
       a)uthor search, B)ody search, c)atchup, f)ollowup, K=mark read,
       |=pipe, m)ail, o=print, q)uit, r)eply mail, s)ave, t)ag, w=post

                                              --More--(81%) [1313/1603]


AA  CD  OH  RD  SD  TR  MR       Connected 10:25        9600 8N1    6:11pm 08/19
```

screen. The **tin** program uses the **more** paging facility, so the word More and the percentage of text that has been read in an article appear at the bottom of the page.

Navigating Articles

Many of the commands for navigating articles are the same as the ones for moving through newsgroups and threads. However, a few additional commands are available for navigating articles. The following are navigation commands for moving around articles.

Command	Moves
Spacebar, Ctrl-D, Ctrl-F	Down one page at a time
b, Ctrl-B, Ctrl-U	Up one page at a time
n	To article number *n*
0 (zero), <	To the base article (first article in the thread)
$	To the last page of the article
Up Arrow, k	Up one page
Down Arrow, j	Down one page
>	To the first page of the last article in the current thread
n	To the next article
N, Tab	To the next unread article
p	To the previous article
P	To the previous unread article
q	To the thread level

Marking Articles as Read and Unread

When you read an article, **tin** marks it as read. This means that **tin** updates your **.newsrc** file, so the read article no longer shows up the next time you open the thread. You can mark an article as unread even if you've read it or mark an article as read even if you haven't read it. Here are commonly used commands for marking articles as read or unread.

Command	Effect
z	Marks current article as unread
k	Marks current article as read and advances to next unread article
K	Marks current article as read and advances to next unread thread
c	Marks all articles as read and returns to thread level
C	Marks all articles as read and goes to next unread thread

See No Evil, Read No Evil

Just like the shrink-wrapped erotic magazines at your local 7-Eleven, potentially offensive postings to widely read newsgroups network news are hidden from view. This is done by means of a simple encryption code called *rot13*. The intent of rot13 isn't to keep any information confidential, it simply prevents readers from accidentally seeing something they would rather have avoided. A posting that is encrypted using rot13 is usually flagged in the article listing as (rot13). If an article has been encrypted, it appears as gibberish. To read what is written, decrypt it by pressing **d**. The screen is redrawn to display the readable text. Pressing **d** again toggles rot13 on again for the originally encrypted article.

SEARCHING, SELECTING, AND SAVING THREADS AND ARTICLES

Many of the operations you perform in the thread and article levels are similar. The keystrokes for searching, selecting, and saving threads and articles are identical. Whether the operation takes effect on an article or a thread depends on the level you're in. The following sections explain how to select, search, and save threads or individual articles.

Searching by Subjects, Authors, or Body Text

At the thread or article level, you can search the subject line, the author, or text in the body of a thread or article. Here are the commands for performing these searches.

Command	Searches
/	Forward to match specified text in the Subject line
?	Backward to match specified text in the Subject line
a	Forward to match specified author
A	Backward to match specified author
B	Current thread for specified text in the body of an article

> **TIP:**   If you want to list all the authors of the articles in a selected thread, press **l** (lowercase L, not the number one). This lists the number of lines in each article, the author of each article, and each author's e-mail address. After viewing the list, press **q** to return to the thread listing.

Automatically Selecting Threads

When you press **Ctrl-K** in the thread or article level, the Kill/Auto-select menu appears. The Auto-select menu lets you automatically select threads or articles by text appearing in the subject line or by a specific author. Automatically selected threads or articles are also referred to as *hot* descriptions. To select threads or articles with a specific pattern automatically, change to the appropriate thread or article and do the following:

1. Press **Ctrl-K**. The Kill/Auto-select menu appears.

2. Press **Spacebar** to change the `Kill type` option from `Kill` to `Auto Select` and press **Enter**. The cursor moves to the `Kill text pattern:` field.

3. Specify a search pattern for the subject or author you want to select, and press **Enter**. The cursor moves to the `Apply pattern to:` field.

4. Press **Enter** to choose `Subject line only` if you want to select only text matching the Subject line. Press **Spacebar** to choose the `From line: only` (to specify an author). Press the **Spacebar** twice to choose both the `Subject:` and `From:` lines. Press **Enter** and the cursor jumps to the `Kill pattern scope:` field.

5. Press **Enter** to match the current group only or press **Spacebar** to select `All groups` and press **Enter**. A prompt appears that allows you to edit, quit, or confirm your choices.

6. Press **Enter** to save the hot description. The Subject lines with text matching the hot description appear with an asterisk next to them, indicating they are automatically selected. Press ~ (tilde) to unselect the threads.

FYI: Searching for specific keywords in thread or article Subject lines is a hit-or-miss proposition. Many subject lines don't give specific information on what the article or thread is about.

Mailing Yourself a Thread or Articles

As you read through a thread, you can e-mail a copy of an article, a group of articles, or even the entire thread to yourself or someone else. Whether you're sending an entire thread or multiple articles, each article is sent as a separate message. The following steps explain how to send a thread, multiple articles, or a single article via e-mail.

1. Select the thread or article(s) you want to send. To mail an entire thread, move to the thread level and press **t**. If you want to send more than one article but not all articles in a thread, make sure you are in the article level and tag each article you want by displaying it, then pressing **t**.

2. Press **m**. A prompt appears to confirm what you're mailing. If you're mailing a thread, press **t**. If you're sending an article, press **a**. If you're sending tagged articles, press **T**. The **tin** program prompts you to enter the e-mail address that you want to send the threads or article(s) to.

3. Enter the e-mail address you want to send the thread or article(s) to. The **tin** program displays the prompt q)uit e)dit s)end [*article subject header*]:.

4. Press **s** to send the thread or article(s).

Saving a Thread or Article to a File

To save a thread or article, press **s** followed by a file name at the thread or article level. When you press **s**, the **tin** program displays the Save Filename [ ]> prompt. Enter your chosen file name. The **tin** program displays a prompt similar to this:

```
Save a)rticle, t)hread, h)ot p)attern, T)agged
articles, q)uit: a
```

Press **a** or **Enter** to save a single file or press **t** to save a thread. The **tin** program displays the prompt

```
Process n)one s)hare u)ud, l)ist zoo e)xt zoo, L)ist
zip, E)xt zip, q)uit: n
```

Text articles are uncompressed files. Pressing **Enter** saves the file(s) in your **News** directory. If you're saving a thread, each article is saved as a separate file with the same file name but with a numbered extension. After

saving a thread or article to a file, you can continue
working with threads or articles.

Saving Multiple Articles to Files

You can save multiple articles to files in your **News**
directory. The first step is to tag each article you want to
save by making sure it is currently displayed, then pressing **t**. Move to the next article, then press **t**, and so on
for each article you want to save. Pressing **t** while a
tagged article is displayed untags the article. After tag-
ging the articles, use the **s** command to save them as files.
The **tin** program displays a prompt similar to this:

```
Save a)rticle, t)hread, h)ot pattern, T)agged
articles, q)uit: T
```

Press **Enter**. The **tin** program displays the prompt

```
Process n)one s)hare u)ud, l)ist zoo e)xt zoo, L)ist
zip, E)xt zip, q)uit: n
```

Pressing **Enter** saves each message as a separate file in
your **News** directory.

Saving Binary File Articles

Some of the most popular newsgroups, such as **alt.bina-
ries.pictures** and **comp.binaries.ibm.pc.**, contain binary
files. These are binary pictures and programs that are
encoded and/or compressed. Most of the pictures are in
jpeg and CompuServe's **gif** format. A question users
commonly ask is, How do I get these pictures and how
do I view them? Here's the answer.

   First you need to understand how to read the articles list
for groups containing pictures. Sometimes pictures are too
large to be posted in one message in a newsgroup. Their
file listings appear with bracketed numbers indicating a
series of files. Consider, for example, the following list:

```
1 + explosion.jpg [01/2] Cool Explosion Garth Algar

2 + explosion.jpg [02/2] Cool Explosion Garth Algar

3 + frog.gif Frog Baseball                Eddie Haskell
```

Here the file **explosion.jpg** is made up of two files that need to be saved and processed to create the whole **explosion.jpg** file. If you want to save a file that is posted in multiple parts, move to the first part [1/2] and press **t** to tag the file. Highlight the second part [2/2] and press **t** to tag the second part. If you want to save a single file, simply highlight it. Press **s** to save the file or files. The **tin** program displays a prompt similar to this:

```
Save a)rticle, t)hread, h)ot p)attern, T)agged
articles, q)uit: T
```

If you are downloading a single file, **a** appears as the default; if you are downloading tagged files, **T** appears as the default, as in the prompt example shown. Pressing **Enter** displays the prompt Save filename [ ]>. You can enter a temporary file name that you can change when you save the file. For example, you might enter **temp.tin**. The **tin** program then displays the following prompt:

```
Process n)one s)hare u)ud, l)ist zoo e)xt zoo, L)ist
zip, E)xt zip, q)uit: n
```

Press **u**. Posted binary files are encoded from a binary format to an ASCII representation of the file with the **uuencode** command. The **uuencode** command also adds a header to the encoded file. The u)ud option stands for **uudecode.** Using this option strips the header from the file and decodes the ASCII file back into its original binary format. The **tin** program displays a message similar to this:

```
Uudecoding ...
```

```
Checksum of /usr/beavis/News/explosion.jpg
```

```
21425      357       364689 bytes
```

Delete saved file that has been post processed? (y/n): y

Press **Enter** to save the file and delete the temporary files used to create the file. The file is then stored in your News directory. If you're using a service provider, you will need to download the file to your local computer as explained later.

> **CAUTION:** Discussions that take place in binary groups cause lots of grief and clutter up the binary files group. Be prepared to be roasted if you start a discussion in a binaries, sources, or archive newsgroup. A newsgroup that allows discussions related to the matching binary, source, or archive newsgroups ends with a **.d**.

Working with Compressed Files.   One of the most convenient features of the **tin** program is that it uncompresses **uuencoded**, **.zip**, and **.zoo** files on the fly when a file is saved. Using **tin,** you don't need to have the uncompression program on your system to uncompress the file. Almost all binary files are at least uuencoded. So, if you want to save a binary file that doesn't end with a **.zip** or **.zoo** extension, choose the u)ud option to uudecode the file.

If the file you want to download ends with **.zip** or **.zoo**, choose the option that matches the file name extension. This causes the **tin** program to uudecode and uncompress the file automatically. For example, press **E** to choose the E)xt zip option. This uncompresses files ending with the extension **.zip**. Choosing the e)xt zoo option by pressing **e** uncompresses files ending with **.zoo**. Both the compressed file and the uncompressed file will appear in your **News** directory.

Downloading a File to Your Computer

If you're using a service provider to connect to the Internet and you want the file on your computer, you will need to download the file from your account to your local computer. In most cases, the **sx** command is used to send a single file using the XModem protocol. The **sz** command sends one or more files using the ZModem protocol. ZModem is faster and can download multiple files. If your communications software supports the ZModem protocol, use it. To download a file named **frog.gif** from your account to your local computer using the ZModem protocol, in your home directory enter

```
sz News/frog.gif
```

You can then issue the command from your local communications software to receive the file.

PARTICIPATING IN NEWSGROUPS

There are three ways the **tin** program lets you participate in a newsgroup that you are subscribed to. You can:

- Reply to the author of an article privately via an e-mail message.
- Post a follow-up article, which is added to an existing thread.
- Post a base article that starts a new thread.

Regardless of whether you reply to an author, post a follow-up article, or post a base article, the **tin** program places you in the default text editor for your site's **tin** program after you enter the appropriate command. The default is usually the **vi** editor. You'll need to be able to work in the text editor in order to participate in a newsgroup thread using **tin**. See Chapter 7 for information on how to work with the **vi** and **pico** editors.

FYI: Practice netiquette (as explained in Chapter 1) when participating in newsgroups. Also check for any FAQs (Frequently Asked Questions) postings that provide information about posting articles to newsgroups. FAQs on posting articles can be found in the **news.answers** group. A document containing netiquette guidelines can be found in the newsgroup **news.announce.newusers**. Other document files that share insights on news include *A Primer on How to Work with the USENET Community*, *Hints on Writing Style for USENET*, and *Rules for Posting to USENET*. These files are available via **ftp** at site: rtfm.mit.edu, directory: **/pub/usenet/news.answers**. For information on using **ftp,** see Chapter 5.

Spicing Up Your John Hancock with a Signature File

The **tin** program recognizes a signature stored in either the **.signature** or **.Sig** file in your home directory. A **.signature** file is a text file that contains additional information about you and is appended to the end of an outgoing message. Signature files can contain your full name, postal address, fax number, other e-mail addresses, and so on. Many people like to include a quote. You must use a text editor, such as **vi** or **pico** (see Chapter 7), to create a **.signature** file. The following is a sample signature.

```
-----------------------------------------------------
Beavis                      |
beavis@shell.portal.com     |
(415) 967-0559 voice        |   "Huh-huh, Huh-huh."
(415) 967-8283 fax          |
-----------------------------------------------------
```

If a **.signature** file exists, then the signature will be pulled into the editor by **tin** for any reply, follow-up article, or posting. The signature in the **.signature** file will not be pulled into the editor for posting commands, but it will be appended to the posted message. A signature in **.Sig** will be displayed in the editor for both posting and mailing commands. Only the first four lines of your **.signature** file will be posted when you post using **tin**.

Replying to the Author of an Article

The **tin** program lets you reply by e-mail to the author of an article. Using the **r** command to reply to the author via e-mail automatically loads the original article and the current response and opens the default text editor for your system. The **R** command places you directly in your editor, ready to create a reply, but it excludes the original message. If you need to refer to the original article as you compose your reply, you have to leave the editor.

Posting a Follow-up Article

To submit a follow-up article, use the **f** command. This automatically creates a header that displays your name and address and reprints the original article with lines prefixed by colons (:). It places you in the default editor to edit the existing message and compose your follow-up response. Be sure to edit the copy of the previous article so that you are not sending unnecessary text. Include only a minimum of text, enough so that readers can understand your follow-up message. The **F** command is similar to the **f** command except that it excludes the original article.

Posting an Article

If you're posting a base article to start a new thread, use the **w** command. You can post articles to the current newsgroup from any page in **tin** by pressing **w**, which places you in the default text editor where you create your article. Because you probably don't want your first attempts to appear foolish to thousands of readers, practice posting to the **alt.test** or **misc.test** newsgroup. These groups are specifically created for letting users practice posting articles. The **W** command lists any articles you've posted in a particular thread.

Cross-posting means posting an article to more than one newsgroup. It's usually safe to cross-post to up to three or four groups. To cross-post more than that is considered excessive. To cross-post the current article you've posted, use the **x** command.

After posting or cross-posting an article, you'll receive several replies via e-mail from receiving USENET sites confirming that the article has been posted.

> **FYI:**   If you're using the **pico** editor when posting articles from **tin**, your posting may appear empty. The **tin** program assumes that it can put **+6** before the file name so the editor will start at that line. This works for **vi** but not for **pico** and other editors. Unfortunately **tin** doesn't know this. You have to make a simple configuration change by typing **M** after you enter **tin** and choose option **#2, Editor offset**. By default it is **on.** Turning it **off** resolves the problem.

CUSTOMIZING tin

When you first start **tin**, it creates a **.newsrc** file in your home directory. The **.newsrc** file determines the order in which newsgroups are displayed, and keeps track of what groups you are subscribed to and what articles in each group you've read. Each line in your **.newsrc** file appears similar to this:

```
news.answers: 1-37,51
```

If you are subscribed to a newsgroup, the name is followed by a colon. If you are not subscribed, the name is followed by an exclamation point. The numbers after the newsgroup show which articles in that group have been read. The **tin** program will list newsgroups in the same order in which they appear in the **.newsrc** file. The **.newsrc** file is a text file that can be edited using a text editor. See Chapter 7 for information on how to work with the **vi** or **pico** editor.

Editing the **.newsrc** file can simplify using **tin**. You can unsubscribe from a group by changing : to ! or subscribe to a newsgroup by changing ! to :. You can mark articles as unread by editing the numbers indicating read articles. Additionally you can change the order of the newsgroups in the newsgroup-level listing. The **.newsrc** list of the newsgroups that you don't subscribe to might not be complete; a complete list of newsgroups can be found in the file **/usr/lib/news/active**; most of them are described in the file **/usr/lib/news/newsgroups**. The following steps explain how to edit your **.newsrc** file to subscribe to only the newsgroups you want. It first globally unsubscribes from all newsgroups and explains how you subscribe to groups selectively by replacing ! with :.

> **CAUTION:**   Do not edit your **.newsrc** file while **tin** is running.

1. Enter **vi .newsrc**.

2. Enter **: %s/:/!/** this is a global replace command that turns all colons exclamation points. This unsubscribes you from everything.

3. Find the groups you want to subscribe to, either by using a search command if you know the groups' names (*/groupname*), or by scrolling through the file. You can make broad cuts on the basis of the top-level summaries. When you find a group you want to subscribe to, position the cursor over the ! and type **r:**.

4. Press **Shift-ZZ** to exit **vi**. You will now be subscribed to those groups followed by a colon. If you want to abort your changes, enter **:q!**.

Changing the tin Program's Default Editor

How you change from the default **vi** editor to the **pico** editor depends on whether you're using the Korn shell

or the C shell. To change from the **vi** to **pico** editor, enter
whereis pico to display the full path name of the **pico**
editor. Make a note of the path name. If you're using the
Korn shell, use the **pico** editor to edit the **.profile** file in
your home directory and replace the path name in the line
VISUAL=*pathname* with the path name of the pico editor.

If you're using the C shell, use the **pico** editor to edit
the **.login** file in your home directory to change the
setenv VISUAL *pathname* path name   to the path
name of the pico editor. For example, to change from
the **vi** editor to the **pico** editor using the C shell, you
might change the line **setenv VISUAL/usr/ucb/vi** to
setenv VISUAL/usr/local/bin/pico.

Changing the .tinrc File

The **.tinrc** file in your home directory contains several
customization settings for working with **tin**. These
options can be changed from within **tin** by pressing **M**
in the newsgroup level. This displays the Options Menu
screen. To change an option, enter the number of the
option you want to change. Some of the options are
toggles, which you can change by pressing **Spacebar**.
Other options are path and file names, which you can
change. For example, you can specify a directory
other than **News** for storing downloaded files. Pressing any key other than a numeric key saves your
changes.

The **.tinrc** file can be viewed or edited with a text
editor the same way the **.newsrc** file is edited. Each
option appears in the **.tinrc** file with an explanation
before the option setting. Each of these explanations
begins with a number sign (#), indicating to the **tin**
program that the line of text is a comment and should
not be treated as a command.

LISTSERV: BITNET NEWS VIA E-MAIL

BITNET is a separate, worldwide network with gateways to the Internet, USENET, and other networks. On BITNET there is an automated system of newsgroups called LISTSERV. LISTSERV groups are similar to USENET newsgroups, except that you can participate (read and post articles) in these groups only via e-mail. This is because there is no direct link between the BITNET network and the Internet. Users share information via e-mail with those who subscribe to the newsgroup. You subscribe to a newsgroup on LISTSERV in order to begin receiving e-mail articles sent by that newsgroup's participants. You read these articles as you would any e-mail. Keep in mind that if the newsgroup you subscribe to is active, you'll receive a lot of messages.

> **FYI:** For a complete listing of LISTSERV discussion groups, send an e-mail message to LISTSERV@BITNIC.BITNET and include the line **send netinfo filelist** in the body of the message. For information on working with LISTSERV, send a separate message to the same address with **help** in the body of the message. See Chapter 2 for information on working with e-mail.

Subscribing to and Unsubscribing from a LISTSERV Group

To subscribe to a LISTSERV group, send an e-mail message to the LISTSERV address (see the LISTSERV@*address* column in the table below). For example, to subscribe to the Amnesty International newsgroup, type **LISTSERV@jhuvm.BITNET** in the To: field of your e-mail message. Within the body of the message, type the following:

```
SUBSCRIBE listname yourname
```

Replace *listname* with the name of the list you want (see the SUBSCRIBE *listname* column in Table 3-1) and replace *yourname* with your name as you usually write it. Using the Amnesty International list example again, type **SUBSCRIBE amnesty Beavis**. Don't use your user ID or e-mail address. LISTSERV gets your e-mail address from the message header. Once you've put this command in the body of the message, send it. In most cases, you will receive a welcome message informing you that you are subscribed and giving you additional information about the list. You'll then get e-mail messages about the topic you subscribed to.

To unsubscribe, send another message to the LISTSERV address, but replace the subscribe line in your message with

UNSUB *listname*

The following is a sampling of LISTSERV topics and the corresponding information you need to subscribe to a LISTSERV newsgroup.

Topic	LISTSERV@ *address*	SUBSCRIBE *listname*
Amnesty International	jhumv.BITNET	amnesty
BBS	saupm00.BITNET	bbs-l
Cooking	vtvm2.BITNET	eat-l
Cyberspace	marist.BITNET	cyber-l
DTP	yalevm.ycc.yale.edu	dtp-l
Dieting	ubvm.cc.buffalo.edu	diet
Education	pltumk11.BITNET	appl-l
English	uga.cc.uga.edu	words-l
Film and TV	ua1vm.BITNET	screen-l
Games	brownvm.brown.edu	games-l

Topic	LISTSERV@ *address*	SUBSCRIBE *listname*
Gardening	ukcc.uky.edu	gardens
Genealogy	vm1.nodak.edu	roots-l
History	psuvm.psu.edu	history
Humor	tcsvm	nutworks
Hypercard	purccvm.cc.vm.edu	hypercrd
IBM PCs	vmd.cso.uiuc.edu	i-ibmpc
Mac Apps	dartcms1. dartmouth.edu	macappli
Movies	itesmvf1.BITNET	film-l
MUD Info	uriacc.BITNET	ud-l
Pets	itesmvf1.BITNET	pets-l
Politics	ucf1vm.cc.ucf.edu	POLITICS
Questions and Answers	trearn.BITNET	misc
Rock 'n' Roll	tritu.BITNET	rock
Travel	trearn.bitnet@vm1. nodak.edu	travel-l
Violence	bruspvm.BITNET	violen-l
Viruses	lehiibm.bitnet@cunyvm. cuny.edu	virus-l
Weather	vmd.cso.uiuc.edu	wx-misc
Weird	brownvm.brown.edu	weird-l
Windows	UICVM.uic.cc.edu	WIN3-L

Participating in a LISTSERV Discussion

The address that you send e-mail to when you participate in a discussion is different from the LISTSERV e-mail address. In other words, commands are sent to the LISTSERV address and discussion messages are sent to another address, called the *list address*. The list address is the same as the SUBSCRIBE *listname* field followed by the last part of the LISTSERV address (the part after LISTSERV@). Say, for example, you subscribe to

nutworks; in order to send a discussion message, you send e-mail to the address **nutworks@tcsvm**. If you subscribe to the **weird-1** list, you send e-mail to **weird-l@brownvm.brown.edu**.

Chapter 4

INTERACTIVE INTERNET

The Internet highway is dotted with hundreds of interactive roadside attractions and services, including online library catalogs, databases, games, party-line discussions, and virtual communities. Many of these are publicly accessible at no charge. The Telnet protocol is the basis for remote login services for computers connected to the Internet. The **telnet** program is the vehicle that lets you work on another computer via remote control. In this chapter we explain how to harness your **telnet** powers to visit all kinds of useful and interesting sites.

REMOTE CONTROL COMPUTING USING TELNET

When you make a connection using the **telnet** program, your computer becomes the *client*, the system requesting the service via remote control. The remote computer is referred to as a *server* or *host*, which runs the programs you request. On UNIX systems, a server is also referred to as a *daemons*. Once you're connected to a host computer, you use the commands native to the host computer to access information and run programs. What is allowed on that host computer depends on the privileges assigned to the account you use to login to that computer. In most cases, you don't need to have a private account on the host computer. Instead, you'll be able to use a guest account with guest privileges.

> **FYI:**   Some telnet host computers run on IBM mainframes, requiring you to use a different version of **telnet** called **tn3270** (if it exists on your system) in order to emulate an IBM 3270 terminal. It is similar to the **telnet** program, though the keys may not correspond exactly. In most cases you will not need to use the **tn3270** program, because most host computers on the Internet are UNIX based.

SURVEYING THE TELNET SERVICES TERRAIN

There is a vast array of resources on the Internet that you can access via **telnet.** Most of these services fall into the following categories.

- Online library catalogs are electronic card catalogs for searching and viewing a library's bibliographical records. Several hundreds of these catalogs are available, mostly at academic institutions.
- Online databases run the range of topics from the practical, such as world news, to the esoteric, such as enzyme databases.
- Bulletin board systems (BBSs) are similar to PC bulletin boards that can be connected to by a modem. Many of these BBSs not only provide information resources but also provide e-mail and conferencing capabilities.
- Freenets are community-based bulletin board systems with e-mail, information services, interactive communications, and conferencing. Freenets are funded and operated by individuals and volunteers—much like public television.
- Campus Wide Information Systems (CWIS) provide campus-specific information such as event calendars, newsletters, available jobs, athletic and cultural events, and course catalogs. Most of this information is not of

interest to outsiders, however CWIS does provide links to useful databases and online library catalogs.

- UNIX-based servers are available to the public for working on a UNIX system. With them you can perform a wide range of computing activities, such as running programs and sending e-mail to users on the local network.

PINPOINTING TELNET SITES

A number of resources are available for finding telnet site addresses. You can get text files that list telnet sites by using the **ftp** program (see Chapter 5). Or you can access online databases using the **telnet** program. One of the most popular of these is the **hytelnet** program, which is explained in the next section. You can also download DOS, Windows, or Macintosh help files to your computer. These provide hypertext-like help for displaying listings of telnet sites. The following list provides some popular telnet site addresses. They give you a sampling of the main categories of telnet sites.

> **TIP:** You can save telephone charges with **telnet** if you have an account with an online service such a CompuServe or DELPHI. To telnet to CompuServe, enter **telnet HERMES.MERIT.EDU**. When prompted for a system, enter **CompuServe**. To telnet to DELPHI, enter **telnet delphi.com**.

Telnet Site Address

Online library catalogs	Description
hollis.harvard.edu	Harvard University. A tn3270 site.
lib.dartmouth.edu	Dartmouth University.
locis.loc.gov	Library of Congress Information System.

Telnet Site Address

Online library catalogs	Description
melvyl.ucop.edu	University of California MELVYL System.
nyplgate.nypl.org	New York Public Library.

Online databases

info.rutgers.edu	Rutgers University CWIS provides world news, weather, dictionary, thesaurus, and CIA World Factbook.
pac.carl.org	Colorado Alliance of Research Libraries (CARL) Public Access Catalog of services, library databases, online encyclopedia, book reviews, etc.

Bulletin board systems,

fdabbs.fda.gov Login: bbs	Food and Drug Administration BBS that provides information on the current activities of the FDA, such as recently approved drugs.
spacemet.phast.umass.edu Login: guest	SpaceMet Internet is a BBS supported by the University of Massachusetts (Amherst) covering space-related topics and other topics including an online version of *USA Today*.

Freenets

freenet-in-a.cwru.edu freenet-in-b.cwru.edu freenet-in-c.cwru.edu	Cleveland Freenet.

Telnet Site Address

Online library catalogs	Description
heartland.bradley.edu Login: bbguest	Heartland Freenet.
yfn.ysu.edu Login: visitor	Youngstown Freenet.

Campus-Wide Information Systems

psupen.psu.edu
  Login: two-letter
  abbreviation for your
  state
	News articles, fact sheets, and reports on agricultural and consumer topics provided by the College of Agricultural Sciences at Pennsylvania State University.

cuinfo.cornell.edu 300	Cornell University CWIS.
techinfo.mit.edu	MIT University CWIS.

Public access UNIX

nyx.cs.du.edu Login: guest	University of Denver UNIX server.

hermes.merit.merit.edu
  Enter: um-m-net
  Enter: g (guest)
  Login: newuser
	Michigan Network.

FYI: The **Dir10** DOS and Windows help programs list telnet sites and other resources on the Internet. These programs are available via **ftp** at site: **ftp.uwp.edu**, directory: **/pub/msdos/dir**, file: **ddir10.zip** (DOS) or **wdir10.zip** (Windows). A listing of libraries and databases is available via **ftp** at site: **csd4.csd.uwm.edu**, directory: **/pub**, file: **inet.services.txt**. An extensive listing of online library card catalogs is available via **ftp** at site: **ftp.oit.unc.edu**, directory: **pub/docs/lib-cat-alogs.online**, file: **LIBRARIES.TXT**. See Chapter 5 for information on using the **ftp** program.

Finding Sites with hytelnet

The **hytelnet** program is a menu-based program that helps you find Internet-accessible libraries, Freenets, CWIS, Library BBSs, and other information sites. It's a hypertext-like tool for users with a dedicated Internet connection from an IBM-compatible PC. This version not only finds a telnet site but also makes the connection for you. If you're connecting to the Internet through a service provider, the **hytelnet** program is still useful for finding site addresses while you're offline. After you look up the address you can then make your telnet connection.

There is an online UNIX version of **hytelnet** that will also initiate connections to remote systems. To access the online UNIX **hytelnet** program enter

```
telnet access.usaak.ca
```

and login as **hytelnet**.

> **FYI:** To get the PC version of the **hytelnet** program, use the **ftp** program (see Chapter 5) to access the ftp site: **ftp.usask.ca**, directory: **pub/hytelnet/pc**, file: **hytelnet65.zip** The **hytelnet** files are archived using the PKZIP utility.

GETTING STARTED WITH TELNET

Entering **telnet** at your local system prompt without a host computer address starts the **telnet** program, putting you in what is referred to as the *command mode*. The `telnet>` prompt appears, indicating you can enter **telnet** commands.

Before you make a telnet connection, you can display a list of commands and settings using the **help** and **display** commands, so you can become familiar with the commands you might need to use. In the command mode, typing **help** or a question mark (**?**) displays a list of the **telnet** commands available on your client computer. The listing includes a brief description of each command. To display a listing of your **telnet** program settings, type **display**. This displays the key sequences used by your **telnet** program to suspend the connection.

Making a telnet Connection

The **telnet** program allows you to make a connection in two ways. If you're already in the command mode, at the telnet prompt, type

```
open host-computer-address
```

where *host-computer-address* is the Internet address of the telnet site. The *host-computer-address* can be specified with either the domain name address or the numeric IP address. For example, typing **open spacelink.msfc.nasa.gov** or **open 192.149.89.61** connects you to the NASA Spacelink database.

If you're not in the **telnet** program, at your system prompt type

```
telnet host-computer-address
```

After connecting to the host computer, you're usually greeted with information about the telnet site. The user name and password for gaining public access to the host system are often displayed in the first screen you see after you make the initial connection. Enter the user name and password.

Sometimes when you login to a host computer, you'll be asked about your terminal type. If you are in doubt, specify VT-100, which is the most common terminal emulator. Terminal emulation makes your PC appear as a standard ASCII terminal to the host system.

> **FYI:**   The host computer usually informs you how to logout or terminate your telnet connection. Look for this information when you start a session and note it in case it's not posted when you want to logout.

Port Numbers in telnet Addresses

At some telnet sites, you need to specify an additional identifier, called a *port number*, in the host computer's address. The port identifier helps to keep separate the many services running on a host computer. For example, entering **telnet culine.colorado.edu 859** specifies the port for the telnet host computer that lists the NBA basketball schedules and entering **telnet culine.colorado.edu 863** specifies the port that lists football schedules.

GETTING AROUND ON THE HOST COMPUTER

Once you're connected to a host computer, you use the commands native to the host computer. How easy it is to get around on the host computer depends on who is maintaining the computer. Many telnet host computers provide a friendly menu system to simplify working on them. Other systems require you to enter commands, which in most cases are UNIX commands. Special function keys and **Ctrl** key combinations are local implementations that can vary from those on your local system.

> **FYI:** If a host computer requires you to use UNIX commands, see Chapter 7 for an overview of commonly used UNIX commands.

MAKING A BREAK FROM THE HOST COMPUTER

Many telnet sites support *breaks*. A break is an instruction to interrupt whatever the host computer is currently doing without terminating the telnet connection. Using a break lets you get out of something you don't want to do on the host computer. For example, after executing a search command, you may realize it's not what you wanted. Pressing a break key sequence tells the host computer to stop the search. When you send a break, your local **telnet** program receives your break and sends out a character sequence that is reinterpreted on the other end, ideally as the break you intended.

There is no one standard break key sequence across telnet host computers. Different host computers recognize different break key commands. Your break might not always be understood by the remote system. The most common UNIX break key sequence is **Ctrl-C**.

> **CAUTION:** Don't go crazy pressing the break key. Too many breaks can cause your telnet connection to be terminated.

GETTING BACK TO YOUR COMPUTER DURING A CONNECTION

Once you've established a telnet connection, all the commands you type are sent to the host computer for execution. If you're in the middle of a telnet session and want to execute a **telnet** or other command on your local client computer, first *escape* out of the telnet connection back to your local **telnet** prompt. Escaping the connection does not terminate the connection.

On most UNIX-based computers, the escape sequence is **Ctrl-]**. After pressing the escape sequence, press **Enter** to return to your local client computer's operating environment. Using the escape sequence brings you back to the telnet command mode on your client computer. Once you're in the command mode, you can use the **z** command to exit the **telnet** program temporarily and get back to the system prompt so that you can execute other commands on your client computer. The telnet connection remains open while you work at your client computer. When you're done working on your client computer, you can return to the telnet command mode by typing **fg** (foreground) at the system prompt. Press **Enter** to reestablish your connection to the host computer.

> **FYI:**   You can find out what the escape sequence is for your
> system by entering **display** at the telnet prompt on your
> client computer.

Changing the Escape Setting

It's important that your escape character be a character that
you'll never need to type in your normal work using the
telnet program. If your **telnet** program's escape character
clashes with a host computer command, you can change
your escape character setting. You do this with the **telnet**
program's **set** command. For example, typing

```
set escape characters
```

sets the escape sequence to the specified *characters*. For
example, to change the default escape sequence from
Ctrl-] to **Ctrl-[**, type **set escape ^[**. You can press **Ctrl**
or caret (^).

LOGGING OUT OF THE HOST COMPUTER

Most telnet host computers let you logout of their
systems with a menu item choice or a command. For
example, the menu on the host computer can instruct
you to press **g** (goodbye) or require you to enter a
logout command. Common logout commands include:
bye, **exit**, **quit**, **logout**, **logoff**, **goodbye**, **stop**, and
disconnect.

HELP, I'VE CONNECTED AND CAN'T GET OUT

In a perfect Internet world, you should be able to say
your goodbyes and go your separate way from a host
computer. Unfortunately, it's not always that simple. In
fact, one the most common problems using **telnet** is
terminating the connection. If you can't terminate the
telnet session by logging out of the host computer, you
need to escape back to your client computer to be in the
telnet command mode, then execute a **telnet** command

to terminate the connection. To terminate a connection from your client computer, do the following:

1. Press **Ctrl-]** or the escape sequence for your **telnet** program. This suspends your telnet connection and returns back to telnet command mode on your client computer.

2. Type **quit** or **bye** at the telnet prompt. This logs out of the host computer and returns you to the system prompt.

3. If your telnet connection does not terminate, try **close**. As a last resort, type **abort**. This terminates the connection but leaves the port on the host computer open for an indefinite period.

> **FYI:**   Remember that you can check the command to terminate a telnet connection from your client computer by typing **help** or the question mark (**?**) at the telnet prompt.

INTERNET CB USING IRC

The Internet Relay Chat (IRC) is the CB of the Internet. It lets you participate in interactive discussions with other users online by typing messages back and forth. IRC is a multichannel network that a group of people can use to exchange messages. Each channel has a particular topic. Each person sees the discussion as it takes place and can chat on multiple channels or to a single person. Users are usually identified by a nickname, although anyone can determine another user's real login name. When you join a discussion, an announcement that you have joined will be sent to everyone currently in the group. Another message will be sent when you leave the group. The text you type is sent to the others on your channel as soon as you press return.

Many service providers include IRC as part of their service packages. You can also access IRC sites using the **telnet** program; few sites are publicly available, however. The most likely telnet-accessible IRC sites are Freenets. To access the IRC program using a service provider, you typically type **irc** at the system prompt or choose it from a menu. Whether you're using a service provider or not, you can telnet to a Freenet or another site that offers IRC service. Once connected, you can issue an IRC command by first pressing the slash character (/) followed by the command. The following are some of the most common IRC commands.

> **FYI:** The newsgroup **alt.irc** includes information about IRC sites and other related information. Chapter 3 explains how to work with newsgroups.

Command	Description
/help	Displays IRC commands and other information
/list-public	Lists public channels that are available
/join #*duck*	Joins a discussion group named duck
/join 0(zero), or /unjoin	Leaves the current discussion channel
/nick *new nickname*	Changes your nickname
/*msg nickname text*	Sends a message to a user on your channel
/who #*channel*	Lists everyone on a given channel
/whois *nickname*	Shows the true identity of a user

PLAYING MUD GAMES

There are sites on the Internet that let you play real-time, interactive games. These games range from chess to complex adventure, role-playing games or simulations referred to as MUDs (Multi-User Dungeons). MUDs are patterned after Dungeons and Dragons. You meet other dungeon explorers and wander through a simulated dungeon. While wandering, you might meet other groups, fight monsters, and find treasures. These games are a world of their own and demand an intense learning process to figure out. If you're connected via a service provider, you're at a disadvantage if other players are using a computer with a direct connection to the Internet because the speed with which they can react is faster than the speed of your modem link to the Internet.

FYI: For more information on MUDs, see the network newsgroup **rec.games.mud**. Working with newsgroups is explained in Chapter 3. A listing of MUDs is also available via **ftp** at site: **caisr2.caisr.cwru.edu**, directory: **/pub/mud**. **The Dir10** help program mentioned earlier in this chapter also includes information on MUDs.

Chapter 5

MINING FILES ON THE INTERNET

*T*he Internet is a gold mine of information. Gigabyte after gigabyte of documents, programs, graphics, and other files are stuffed in public file archives. These publicly accessible file mother lodes are scattered throughout the Internet. Anyone can stake a claim to these files; they're free for the grabbing. This chapter explains how to mine the Internet using the **ftp** program.

DIGGING UP FILES WITH FTP

FTP stands for File Transfer Protocol, which is the medium that lets you transfer files among computers across the Internet, regardless of their operating systems. The **ftp** program, named after its protocol, is similar to a mining ore car. It's the vehicle that lets you download and upload files. Some nuances of the **ftp** program change with each operating system, but the basic command structure is the same. The **ftp** program is standard fare on most client computers connected to the Internet. If you're using a service provider, **ftp** is usually available as part of the service package.

Many organizations connected to the Internet provide publicly accessible file archive sites. These public file archives are referred to as *anonymous ftp* sites. The term anonymous refers to a generic account that can be used by anyone to login to an ftp host computer. Otherwise, in order to make an ftp connection, you must have an account on the ftp host computer.

> **FYI:** Anonymous ftp sites are a public service provided by many of the organizations connected to the Internet. As a courtesy to these organizations, avoid using ftp sites during the busy daytime hours (6:00 A.M. to 7:00 P.M. remote site time). Use anonymous ftp sites at night or on weekends, when the organizations' own demands on these computing resources are low.

PROSPECTING FOR ANONYMOUS FTP SITES

Hundreds of anonymous ftp sites are available for prospecting on the Internet. Different sites can have different veins of files. For example, some sites cater to UNIX users and some cater to Mac or Windows users. As you travel the Internet, over time you'll discover new ones from a variety of sources. You can access lists of anonymous ftp sites by downloading and using widely available help programs for Windows and the Macintosh. The quickest way to find anonymous ftp sites is to use the **ftp** program to download a text file containing a list of anonymous ftp sites. For starters, the following list is a sampler of popular ftp sites that you can visit and download files from using the **ftp** commands explained in this chapter.

> **FYI:** A list of anonymous ftp sites is available via **ftp** at site: **pilot.njin.net**, directory: **/pub/ftp-list,** file: **ftp.list**. This listing is also available on many other anonymous ftp sites. The **Dir10** DOS and Windows help programs also list anonymous ftp sites and other information on the Internet. To get either of these programs, ftp to site: **ftp.uwp.edu,** directory: **/pub,** file: **ddir10.zip** (DOS) and **wdir10.zip** (Windows).

Site	Types of Files	Directories
coe.montana.edu	Television Shows Archive	pub/TV and pub/STARTREK
cs.uwp.edu	UNIX software	/pub/gnu
	Music-related files such as lyrics, interviews with musicians, etc.	/pub/music
csd4.csd.uwm.edu	Internet Service Guide	/pub File: inet.services.txt
ftp.cs.widener.edu	Simpsons Archive	/pub/simpsons
ftp.eff.org	Electronic Magazine (Unplastic News)	/pub/journals/Unplastic_News
ftp.nisc.sri.com	Request For Comments (RFC)	/rfc
ftp.uu.net	List of UUNET ftp archive sites	/index File: ls-lR.Z
	Information on the Clairinet News service	/Clairinet
ftphost.nwnet.net	Internet Resource Guide	/nic/nenet/user-guide File: nusirg
gatekeeper.dec.com	Recipes	/pub/recipes
mrcnext.cso.uiuc.edu	Electronic Books, such as *Alice's Adventures In Wonderland*, works of Shakespeare, *Moby Dick*, etc.	/etext (/etext91 /etext92 /etext93)
prep.ai.mit.edu	Software from the GNU project and compendium of network jargon	/pub/gnu
pit-manager.mit.edu	Frequently Asked Questions (FAQS)	/pub/usenet
sumex-aim.stanford.edu	Macintosh software	info-mac
ftp.cica.indiana.edu	PC software	/pub/pc and /pub/mac

GETTING STARTED WITH FTP

Entering **ftp** at your local system prompt without a host computer address starts the **ftp** program, putting you in the *command mode*. The ftp prompt appears, indicating you can enter **ftp** commands.

Typing **help** or a question mark (**?**) at the ftp prompt displays a list of commands available on your client computer's **ftp** program. Typing **help** *command* or **?** *command* displays information about the **ftp** command you specify.

Making an ftp Connection

The first step in transferring files is to make the ftp connection between your client computer and the host computer. The **ftp** program lets you make a connection in two ways. If you're already in the command mode, type

```
open host-computer-address
```

where *host-computer-address* is the Internet address of the ftp host computer. This activates the **ftp** program on your client computer and makes the connection. For example to connect to the Electronic Frontier Foundation's anonymous ftp site, type **ftp ftp.eff.org**.

After the connection is established and you're prompted for your user name, type **anonymous**. When you login as anonymous, the ftp site typically prompts you to enter your Internet e-mail address as a password. For example, **beavis@shell.portal.com**. If you don't have an Internet e-mail address, type **guest**. As you type your password, the characters don't appear on the screen. This is a security precaution inherent on most computer systems on the Internet. Once you've identified yourself to the remote host computer, an introductory screen usually appears, followed by the ftp prompt.

If you're not in the ftp command mode, at your shell prompt, type

```
ftp host-computer-name
```

to make a connection.

> **FYI:** You can find out where files are located at anonymous ftp sites by using the treasure-hunting **archie** or **gopher** programs. Chapter 6 explains how to use these programs.

NAVIGATING THE FTP HOST COMPUTER

Most computer systems use a hierarchical file structure. Think of an inverted tree with the base of the tree at the top. It's similar to the structure of a family tree. When you login to an ftp host computer, you're at the root directory. The root directory is indicated as a slash (/) on UNIX systems. Subdirectories are listed with a slash (/) before the directory name; for example, **/pub**. Each subsequent directory down in the hierarchy is listed with a slash; for example, **/pub/music/rocknroll**.

This listing of directories is referred to as a *path name*. A path name tells the operating system which paths to take to find a specific directory or file. For example, entering the path name **/usr/beavis** after the **cd** command (**cd /usr/beavis**) instructs the operating system to change to the **beavis** subdirectory, located in the directory named **usr**.

> **FYI:** Keep in mind that directory and file names on UNIX systems are case sensitive. Always type the characters in the case they appear in on your screen.

The **ftp** program includes a few built-in commands for navigating directories. In most cases, these are the same as UNIX commands. Here are common **ftp** commands for navigating directories that you can enter at the ftp prompt.

Command	Action
ls (list)	Lists names of files in the current directory
dir (directory)	Lists more or the same information as the **ls** command
cd *directory* (change directory)	Changes to the directory you specify
cdup (change directory up) or cd ..	Moves up one directory level
pwd (print working directory)	Displays the current directory name

Listing the contents of a directory using the **ls** or **dir** command displays all the files and directories in the working directory. To navigate directories, you need to distinguish directories from files in a listing. File names and directory names are listed on the far right. On the far left are permissions indicating the access privileges for any file or directory (permissions are explained later in this chapter). The letter **d** in the first column of permissions indicates the entry is a directory. Files are indicated by a hyphen (-). To navigate to a directory, type **cd** *directory*. For more information on directory listings, see Chapter 7.

ftp and Non-UNIX Systems

Not all ftp sites are UNIX based; in some cases the ftp site runs on an IBM PC or IBM PC compatible, a Macintosh, or an IBM/VMS system. If you are on an IBM PC or IBM PC–compatible ftp site, you will use DOS rather than UNIX. Instead of the **ls** command, use the **dir** command. To change directories on a PC, use the backslash (\) rather than the slash (/). For example, enter **cd \pubs** instead of **cd /pubs**. The only thing you have to worry about using Macintosh or IBM VM systems is the difference in file name conventions, which is explained later in this chapter in the sections on downloading files.

What's in Here?

Three text files are commonly found on many ftp hosts providing help for exploring anonymous ftp host computers. The **README** file contains information about the archive site or the files within a directory. Directories that include a large number of files sometimes offer an **INDEX** file, which contains information about the files in the directory. Some sites include the file **ls-1R**, which includes a comprehensive listing of all directories and the files included in them that are on the anonymous ftp site. Viewing these files is explained later in this chapter in the section Viewing Text Files on Your Screen.

Controlling a Directory Listing

There is a problem with using the **ls** or **dir** commands during a connection. If the directory listing is longer than a screenful, the listing scrolls right off the screen. Unless you're an incredibly fast speed reader, it's hard to read the scrolling list. To have the directory listing display one screenful at a time, type

```
ls pathname |more
```

Be careful that you don't include a space between the pipe (|) symbol and the **more** command. The pipe symbol sends the output from the **ls** command to the **more** paging facility. *You must enter the full path name and enter a space before |more*. If you don't know the full path name of the directory you're currently in, type **pwd** to display the path name. The **more** paging facility displays one screenful of text at a time. To display the next screenful of information, press the **Spacebar**. Pressing **Enter** displays only the next line. You can exit the listing at any time by typing **q**.

Saving a Directory Listing to a File

The output of the **ls** or **dir** commands can be redirected to an ASCII text file on your client computer instead of having it displayed on your screen. For example, to save the listing of files generated by the **ls** command, type

```
ls pathname filename
```

where *pathname* is the name of the directory on the host computer and *filename* is the name of the text file on your client computer. For example, if you enter the directory **/pub** and the file name **lspub**, the **ftp** program usually displays this prompt

```
output to local-file: lspub?
```

Press **y** to save the file on your computer. You can view and work with the text file on your computer as you would any text file.

Specifying Files in a Directory Listing

You can specify what files you want to appear in a directory by using the asterisk (*****) and question mark (**?**) wild cards. The question mark indicates any single character and the asterisk indicates any group of characters. For example, typing

```
ls *.txt
```

displays only files ending with the extension **.txt**. To list files starting with the letters **un**, type **ls un***. To specify any three-letter file names that begin with the characters hu, type **hu?**, which finds files with three-letter names such as **hug** and **hub.** You can use more than one question mark in a file name. For example, you can type **hu??** to search for any file that starts with hu followed by any two characters, such as **huge** and **hull.** A directory listing can be saved to a file. For example, **ls t* tfiles** saves the directory listing of all the files beginning with **t** in a file named **tfiles** on your client computer.

Viewing Text Files on Your Screen

Text files can be opened during an ftp session to view what's inside them. To view a text file online one screenful at a time, use the **get** command with the **more** paging facility.

```
get filename |more
```

Remember, don't include a space between the pipe (|) and the **more** command. The pipe sends the output from the **get** command to the **more** command so the text file is opened and the first screenful of the file appears on your screen. At the bottom of the screen is the message **more**, indicating you're using the **more** paging facility. To move to the next page of the file, press the **Spacebar**. Pressing **Enter** displays only the next line. You can quit displaying the text file at any time by typing **q**.

IDENTIFYING FILES ON AN FTP HOST COMPUTER

The Internet is a melting pot for all kinds of computer systems and file types. One of the key skills you need to mine files is to know how to identify the different types of files on the Internet. Two main categories of file types exist on the Internet: ASCII and binary. An *ASCII* file is a text file. A text file is the lowest format in the file format food chain. Regardless of the computer you're using, you can read ASCII files, even online. A *binary* file is a file that is encoded with control characters. These files include programs and files that can be used only by specific programs.

It's important that you identify files to make sure they can work on your computer before you download them. Also, many files are compressed to save disk space on the host computer and save disk space and transfer time. To work with these files you need to know which program to use to uncompress the file.

Fortunately, naming conventions exist that help you identify different file types, their compression status, and the compression utility used. Here is a list of the common

file name extensions and the utility programs you need
to uncompress the files.

File name Extension	Operating System	ASCII/ Binary	Compression Utility or File Type
arc	DOS	binary	arc 6.02, pk361
com	DOS	binary	executable file
cpt	Macintosh	ASCII	Compactor 1.21
doc	any	ASCII	text file
exe	DOS	binary	executable file
gif	any	binary	graphics file
gz	UNIX	binary	gzip
hqx	Macintosh	ASCII	BinHex 4.0
jpg	any	binary	graphics file
lzh	DOS	binary	lh113c.exe
mpg	any	binary	video file
pict	Macintosh	binary	picture file
pit	Macintosh	ASCII	PackIt3.1.3
ps	any	ASCII	copy file to PostScript printer
sea	Macintosh	ASCII	self-extracting archive
sh	UNIX	ASCII	unshar (UNIX command)
sit	Macintosh	ASCII	Stuffit, Stuffit Deluxe
tar	UNIX	binary	tar (UNIX command)
tif	any	binary	graphics file
txt	any	ASCII	text file
uu	UNIX	ASCII	uudecode (UNIX command)
wp	DOS	binary	WordPerfect file
Z	UNIX	binary	uncompress (UNIX command)
zip	DOS	binary	PKZIP/PKUNZIP
zoo	UNIX	binary	Zoo

Compression Utilities

Many files on anonymous ftp host computers are compressed to save storage space and reduce the time it takes to transfer files across the Internet. A text file run through a data compression program can be reduced anywhere from 30 to 70 percent in size.

You must uncompress the files to make them usable. There is no one standard for compression; consequently, a number of different compression programs are used. Most compressed files are flagged by a unique extension to let you know the files are compressed (see preceding table). This gives you a hint about what utility should be used to uncompress it. The program you need to uncompress the file will vary depending on what kind of computer you're using and the compression program that was used. The following list contains the most common file compression utilities.

FYI: A guide to compression programs that includes less common archiving and compression software programs can be obtained via **ftp** at site: **ftp.cso.uiuc.edu**, directory: **/doc/pcnet**, file: **compression**.

Compression Utility	DOS	Macintosh	UNIX
ARC (DOS)	arc602.exe	ArcMac1.3c	arc5521
btoa (UNIX)	atob11.zip	no equivalent	btoa
BinHex4.0 (Mac)	xbin23.zip	BinHex4.0	mcvert
compress (UNIX)	u16.zip	MacCompress3.2	uncompress
cpio (UNIX)	pax2exe.zip	no equivalent	cpio
GNU	gzip123.exe	no equivalent	gunzip
LHarc (DOS)	lh113c.exe	MacLHarc 0.41	lharc102
pack (UNIX)	no equivalent	no equivalent	unpack
PackIt (Mac)	UnPackit	Packit3.1.3	unpit
PKZIP (DOS)	pkz204g.exe	UnZip.1	unzip50

Compression Utility	DOS	Macintosh	UNIX
Stuffit/ StuffItLite (Mac)	unsit30.zip	StuffItLite	unsit
tar (UNIX)	tar.zip	UnTar2.0	tar
uuencode (UNIX)	toaduu20.zip	uutool2.0.3	uudecode
zoo (UNIX)	zoo210.exe	MacBooz2.1	zoo

Many sites combine and compress files using the UNIX tar and compress commands. The tar program, by the way, stands for tape archive and is used to combine several compressed files into one file. Files compressed with the compress command end with a .Z. Files that have been compressed and archived with tar end with tar.Z. To uncompress a file that ends with .tar.Z, first use the uncompress command (uncompress filename.tar.Z). This uncompresses the file and removes the .Z extension. You can then enter the command tar -fvx filename.tar to unarchive the file.

> **TIP:** If your client computer is UNIX based, you can use the **zcat** command to view the contents of a compressed file. These compressed files end with the **.Z** extension. For more information on using the **zcat** command see Chapter 7.

Getting File Compression Utilities

You need to download the compression utility program appropriate to your computer using the **ftp** program. If you're accessing the Internet through a service provider, remember that you need to either uncompress the file before you transfer it or uncompress the file after you download the file from the service provider's system to your local computer. This is explained later in this chapter. If you're using a service provider, using an uncompression utility to uncompress the file on your local computer, rather than the service provider's computer, saves you connect and transfer time.

The best way to get a file compression utility is to ftp to the site that stores files for the type of computer you're using. If you're using an IBM PC or compatible, you will want to get the PKZIP program first. Most PC files and compression utilities are compressed using PKZIP. The PKZIP program is a self-extracting file. To extract the file, make a directory, copy the program to the directory, and in the directory, at the DOS prompt, enter **pkz204g**. The following is a list of sites that have compression utilities for different computing platforms.

Platform	Site	Directory
PC (DOS)	ftp.cso.uiuc.edu	/pc/exec-pc
Macintosh	sumex-aim.stanford.edu	/info-mac/util
UNIX	wuarchive.wustl.edu	/misc/unix and /unix-c/arc-progs

DOWNLOADING AND UPLOADING FILES

The **ftp** program lets you transfer files in two directions. The most common use of **ftp** is to download one or more files from an ftp host computer to your client computer. Many anonymous ftp sites don't allow you to upload files because of the threat of spreading virus-infected files. However, the **ftp** program gives you the tools to upload a file or group of files from your client computer to an ftp host computer that does allow uploading files.

> **FYI:** If you're accessing the Internet through a service provider, files are transferred between the service provider's client computer and the host computer. You must download the files from the service provider's computer to your computer. Likewise, to upload files, the files are first uploaded to the service provider's computer then again to the ftp host computer.

ASCII and Binary File Transfers

The **ftp** program has two modes for transferring files: ASCII (text) and binary. By default, **ftp** assumes you're transferring ASCII files. If you're transferring a program or compressed file, you need to tell the **ftp** program that you're transferring a binary file *before* you transfer the file. To change to the binary transfer mode, at the ftp prompt, type **binary**. The system usually responds with the message Type set to I; the I stands for image or binary. You can switch back to ASCII mode at the ftp prompt by typing **ascii**.

Changing Directories on Your Client Computer

During a connection, **ftp** lets you change directories on your client computer with the **lcd** *directory* command. If you plan on downloading files on a regular basis, create a directory on your client computer to store any files you want to download. The **mkdir** command, explained in Chapter 7, lets you create a directory on your client computer.

Downloading a File

The **get** command allows you to download a single file from the ftp host computer to your client computer. File names on UNIX systems are case sensitive, so if a file name is shown in lowercase, you must type it in lowercase. Downloading and uploading files are similar operations.

1. Change to the directory containing the file you want to download.
2. Type **binary** if you're downloading a binary file. Remember, a compressed file should always be treated as binary file for transfer, even if it's a compressed ASCII text file.
3. Type **get** *source-filename destination-filename*. Where *source-filename* is the name of the file on the host computer and *destination-filename* is the name of the

file for your client computer. Typing the *destination-filename* is optional. If you don't use the *destination-filename*, the same file name is used for the file copied to your client computer.

> **FYI:** Macintosh file names can have spaces in them. To download a Macintosh file that contains spaces in its name, put the entire source file name in quotes and be sure to specify a destination file name (without spaces); for example, **get "Movie List" movies**. File names on IBM VM systems consist of two character strings. The first string is the file name and the second is the file type. To download a file from an IBM VM system, separate the file name from the file type with a period and specify a destination file name; for example, **get chapter1.document chap1.doc**.

Downloading Multiple Files

The **mget** command lets you download multiple files at one time. You specify a group of files to be downloaded by matching the characters, using a wild-card character, with file names in the working directory. To download a group of files, type the characters in the file names you want to match followed by an asterisk wild-card character.

```
mget character(s)*
```

For example, to download all files in the current directory that begin with the letter **a**, type **mget a***. All the file names in the directory starting with the letter **a** are downloaded. You can match file extensions by typing

```
mget *.filename-extension
```

For example, typing **mget *.txt** downloads any file in the working directory that ends with the extension **.txt**.

You can verify the number of files matching the search characters by using the **ls** command before you use the **mget** command. If the directory contains a large number of files, you may want to be more specific.

When you download multiple files using the **mget** command, the **ftp** program asks you whether or not you want to download each file before the file is downloaded. Press **y** (yes) then Enter to download the file. Press **n** (no) then Enter to cancel the downloading of the file.

> **TIP:** To save time, you can tell **ftp** not to prompt you to confirm each file being downloaded by typing **prompt** at the ftp prompt before using the **mget** command.

Downloading a File from a Service Provider

If you're using a service provider to access the Internet and you want the file on your computer, you'll need to download the file from your service provider's computer to your local computer. In most cases, the **sx** command is used to send a single file using the XModem protocol. The **sz** command sends one or more files using the ZModem protocol. ZModem is faster and can download multiple files. If your communications software supports the ZModem protocol use it. For example, to download the PKZIP program **pkz204g.exe** from your home directory on the service provider's computer using the ZModem protocol, at the system prompt, enter

```
sz pkz204g.exe
```

and issue the command from your local communications software to receive the file.

Uploading Files

The **put** command lets you upload a single file from your client computer to the ftp host computer. The **mput** command lets you upload multiple files at one time. Remember, to upload a file to an ftp host computer, your account must have uploading permission. Most anonymous ftp sites don't allow uploading of files. Here is how to upload a file.

1. Change to the directory on your client computer containing the file you want to upload.
2. Type **binary** if you're uploading a binary file.
3. Type **put** *source-filename destination-filename*, where *source-filename* is the name of the file on your client computer and *destination-filename* is the name of the file for the ftp host computer. Typing the *destination-filename* is optional. If you don't use the *destination-filename*, the same file name is used.

To specify a group of files to be uploaded, type the characters in the file names you want to match followed by an asterisk (*) wild-card character. You may want to verify the number of files matching the search characters using the **ls** command before you use the **mput** command. For example, to upload multiple files in the current directory that begin with the letter **a**, type **mput a***. All the file names in the directory beginning with the character **a** are uploaded. You can match file extensions by typing

```
mput *.filename-extension
```

If the directory contains a large number of files, you may want to be more specific.

When you upload multiple files using the **mput** command, the **ftp** program asks you whether or not you want to upload each file before it uploads the file. Press **y** (yes) to upload the file. Press **n** (no) to cancel the uploading of the file.

> **TIP:** To save time, you can tell **ftp** not to prompt you to confirm each file being uploaded by typing **prompt** at the ftp prompt before you use the **mput** command.

QUITTING AN FTP SESSION

After you finish your ftp work, you can return home by ending the ftp connection. To terminate the connection

and exit the **ftp** program on your client computer, type
bye. You can also use the **quit** command to end an ftp
session.

GETTING FILES VIA AN FTPMAIL SERVER

You can retrieve files from any anonymous ftp host
computer by placing an e-mail order. This feature, which
allows you to transfer files via remote control without
using the **ftp** program directly, is useful if you don't have
access to the **ftp** program.

In the mail message, you create a simple list of **ftp**
commands to be executed on the anonymous ftp site
you specify. The e-mail message is sent to an ftpmail
gateway called an *ftpmail server*, which processes the
order and e-mails the requested files back to you. You
can request multiple files (up to ten files in a mail
message) from anonymous ftp sites. When making
multiple requests in an e-mail message, keep in mind
that each request is processed in sequence from the
first to final line.

> **FYI:**   Two popular ftpmail servers are **ftpmail@pa.dec.com**
> and **ftpmail@decwrl.dec.com**. You can get complete infor-
> mation about how to use **ftpmail** by sending the single word
> **help** in the body of an e-mail message to an ftpmail server.

Sending an ftpmail Request

Sending an e-mail request to an ftpmail server involves
entering a list of **ftp** commands into a mail message that
mirrors the steps you would actually take to make an ftp
connection yourself. Each line in the e-mail message is
one ftp command sequence. The following steps explain
how to make an e-mail request for a file from an anonymous ftp server using the **pine** mail program (see

Chapter 2). Of course, you can use your own mail program instead of the **pine** program.

1. At the system prompt, type **pine**. The **pine** program's Main Menu screen appears.
2. Press **C**. The Compose Message screen appears.
3. Type **ftpmail@pa.dec.com** in the To: field.
4. In the Subject: field, type in a descriptive subject line to help you identify the return message from the ftpmail server in your mail program's header list.
5. In the Message Text area, type the following:

```
connect csd4.csd.uwm.edu

chdir pub

get inet.services.txt

quit
```

6. Press **Ctrl-X** to send the message.

The message instructs the ftpmail server to connect to the **ftp csd4.csd.uwm.edu** ftpmail server, change to the **pub** directory, get the **inet.services.txt** file, and terminate the ftp connection. The **inet.services.txt** file provides a handy list of ftp and telnet sites.

You'll receive a response from the ftpmail server indicating the status of your request and its place in the server's job queue. The time it takes to receive your request depends on the volume of traffic on the ftpmail server, which can range from a few seconds to a day or two.

FYI: If a message is larger than the default 64K or larger than your mail program can handle, the file is split into as many messages as required for transmission. If you receive your file in pieces, you have to reassemble them in order. Several mail unsplitters are available using **ftp** at site: **gatekeeper.dec.com**, directory: **/pub/mail/ua/misc/unsplit**.

ftpmail Request Commands

The following are common **ftp** commands used in creating ftpmail requests.

Command	Result
connect *hostname* *login password*	Specifies the ftp host to be contacted. Each request in a mail message must have a **connect** statement in it. Login and password are optional. If not given, they default to anonymous and your e-mail address. If you have an account other than anonymous, enter your login name and password in the connect command line.
ascii	Specifies ASCII text files (default).
binary	Specifies the file is binary and should be encoded into ASCII before being transmitted. By default, the file is encoded with the **btoa** utility.
btoa	Specifies that binary files should be encoded with btoa (default).
uuencode	Specifies that binary files should be encoded with **uuencode** rather than **btoa**.
compress, compact	Specifies that binary files should be compressed with the UNIX **compress** or **compact** utility.
chdir *directory*	Changes to the specified directory when the ftp connection is made to the ftp server.

Command	Result
dir, ls *directory*	Displays a directory listing of the specified directory. If no directory is specified, returns a listing of the current directory.
get *filename*	Specifies the file to be sent to you by the ftpmail server.
chunksize *number*	Specifies the maximum number of characters between 10K and 100K that will be sent in any one message. If a message is larger than the number specified (the default is 64K), the file is split into as many messages as required for transmission. After you receive all the pieces, you need to reassemble them in order.
reply *mail-address*	Sets the reply address from the ftpmail server.
quit	Terminates the ftp server connection.

Chapter 6

FINDING WHAT YOU WANT ON THE INTERNET

*T*he Internet is a jungle of sites containing files and other resources. This chapter teaches you how to become the Indiana Jones of the Internet and hack your way through the Internet jungle to find its hidden treasures. It explains the Internet's most powerful tools for finding files and information, including **archie**, **gopher**, **veronica**, WAIS (Wide Area Information Servers), and WWW (World-Wide Web).

USING ARCHIE TO LOCATE FILES

Trekking through the Internet using just the **ftp** program to find a file is like searching for the Holy Grail. In order to get the files you want, you first need to know where the file is. The **archie** program (derived from the word archive) is an online file-finding utility. It doesn't download the files, but it tells you where files reside on anonymous ftp servers. The **archie** program maintains a database of the names of over a million files stored at more than a thousand anonymous ftp sites. The archie server automatically updates the listing information from each site about once a month, ensuring that the information you receive is reasonably up to date. The **archie** program also includes a **whatis** database, which contains descriptions of thousands of public domain software programs and informational documents. The **whatis** database is not kept as up to date as the **archie** database.

You can work with **archie** in one of three ways: by remotely logging into an archie server using **telnet**, using an **archie** program installed on your client computer, or by sending an e-mail message to an archie server. There are a number of archie servers scattered throughout the Internet. As a courtesy to the providers of these servers, if you use **telnet** to connect to an archie server, use the server that is closest to your client computer location. The following is a listing of archie servers serving the United States and Canada.

archie Server	Geographical Area Served (Site Location)
archie.rutgers.edu	Northeastern United States (New Jersey)
archie.sura.net	Southeastern United States (Maryland)
archie.unl.edu	Western United States (Nebraska)
archie.ans.net	Eastern United States (New York)
archie.mcgill.ca	Canada

Connecting to an archie Server via telnet

To start your quest for files, you first need to connect to an archie server in your area using the **telnet** program. Some service providers automatically telnet and connect you to an archie server when you simply enter **archie**. If you enter **archie** on your client computer and a list of options appears, see the section Using **archie** Directly, which follows. Otherwise, to telnet to an archie server, type

```
telnet archie-server-name
```

The archie server displays a standard login prompt. At the login prompt, type **archie**.

You frequently run into crowded conditions on archie servers; in this case, the connection is not made and a message appears telling you to try again later. If you make a connection, the `archie>` prompt appears. At this point, you're in the **archie** program, ready to perform a search. Different servers default to different types of searches. To check how searches are made by the server you're using, enter **show search** at the archie prompt. You can change the search type by entering

set search *type*

where *type* specifies one of the following ways **archie** should conduct your search:

Type	Description
exact	The search string (characters) must exactly match a file name.
regex	The search string is treated as a regular expression to match file name. Usually the default setting.
sub	The search string will match a file name that contains it as a substring. Case is ignored. This is probably the most useful search type for general-purpose use.
subcase	The search string will match a file name that contains it as a part of its name. The case of the matching string must also match.

Searching for Files by Name. The most common way to look for files is to search for file names. To begin a search, enter

prog *searchstring*

where *searchstring* is the name or character pattern of the file name you want to find. Say, for example, you heard about a PostScript viewer program that was in a file named **gs261exe.zip**. Entering **prog gs261exe.zip** at the archie prompt displays a status line similar to this:

```
# matches / % databases searched:   0 / 20%
```

Showing you that the search is in progress, the percentage of the databases searched changes. Be aware the search can take a few minutes. After the search is complete, **archie** displays a list of servers and matching file names, similar to this:

```
Host nctuccca.edu.tw          (140.111.3.21)
Last updated 1:04 13 Jul 1993


  Location: /PC-Windows/CICA-win3/uploads
    FILE -r--r--r-- 1192261 Jun 7 1993   gs261exe.zip


Host sprite.cica.indiana.edu    (129.79.20.17)
Last updated 11:04 5 Jul 1993


  Location: /pub/pc/win3/uploads
    FILE -r--r--r-- 1192261 Jun 7 19:08   gs261exe.zip


Host terra.stack.urc.tue.nl    (131.155.2.71)
Last updated 01:06 6 Jul 1993


  Location: /pub/nfs/pc/win3/uploads/JUN93
    FILE -r--r--r-- 1192261 Jun 7 19:08   gs261exe.zip
```

This list includes the ftp server address, the last time the file was updated, the file location (path), and the file information (including permissions). Sometimes a search will match a name in a directory path, but not a file name in that directory. Make a note of the address and path information so you can use the **ftp** program to get the file. You can enter another search text pattern or type **quit** to leave **archie** and terminate the telnet session.

Using archie Directly

Some service providers let you use the **archie** program directly. Of course, you can also use **archie** directly if you're using a dedicated Internet connection and have the **archie** program installed. Either way, you can perform searches without having to use the **telnet** program. The syntax for working with a local **archie** program is

```
archie -modifier(s) string
```

The *modifier(s)* control the type of search and *string* indicates the characters to search for. Multiple modifiers can be used, but each must begin with a hyphen; for example, **archie -s -m10**. Here a list of common modifiers.

Modifier	Description
-c	Specifies a case-sensitive search — upper- and lowercase letters must match exactly.
-e	Specifies an exact match — the search string must match exactly (the default). If used with any of the other search modifiers, an exact match is tried before the more time-consuming search types are performed.
-r	Indicates the search string is a regular expression.
-s	Specifies to ignore the case of letters.
-l	Lists one match per line so the output is suitable for input into another program.
-o *filename*	Specifies to store results in *filename*.
-h *name*	Instructs the archie client to use the specified *name* of the host for the request. With many clients you can set an environment variable to have **archie** default to a specific server. On UNIX, set the **ARCHIE_HOST** variable in your **.cshrc** or **.profile** file.

Modifier	Description
-m *number*	Restricts the number of displayed matching files. If you don't specify a *number*, **archie** returns at most 95 matches.

> **FYI:** Client software for **archie** is available for DOS, Macintosh, and UNIX via **ftp** at site: **ftp.unl.edu**, directory: **/pub/archie/clients**.

Using archie via E-mail

You can use **archie** via e-mail by sending a request containing commands for an archie search to be performed on the server. This capability is useful if you don't have **archie** or **telnet** available on your computer. Using **archie** via e-mail lacks some of the options available when the **archie** program is used directly, but it does **archie**'s main job — locating precious files tucked away in the recesses of the Internet.

Creating archie Mail Orders.   Creating an e-mail request to an archie server involves entering a list of **archie** commands into a mail message that mirrors the steps you would actually take to perform the search yourself. Each line in the e-mail message is one archie command sequence. Any command that is not understood is interpreted as a request for help. So if you do anything wrong, you get a help guide returned to you, whether you want it or not.

Here is how to create a request for an archie mail help guide and a list of all known archie servers. This example uses the **pine** mail program (see Chapter 2 for more information on **pine**). Of course, you can use your own mail program instead of **pine**.

1. At the system prompt, type **pine**. The **pine** program's Main Menu screen appears.

2. Press **C**. The Compose Message screen appears.

3. In the To: field, type **archie@archie.unl.edu**.

4. In the Subject: field, type in a descriptive subject line. For example, **Archie request for help and servers**. This is optional, but filling it in lets you easily identify the return e-mail message from the archie server.

5. In the Message Text area, type the following:

   ```
   help

   servers

   quit
   ```

6. Press **Ctrl-X** and press **Enter** to send the message. The e-mail message is sent to the archie server at the University of Nebraska. Sometime later you will receive a reply from the server containing the results of your request.

The following are the commands available to you for sending an archie e-mail request.

Command	Description
path *e-mail-address*	Instructs **archie** to send the responses to the specified *e-mail-address*, rather than the address given in the From field of the requesting e-mail message. This command is useful if you are traversing e-mail gateways and not enough information is conveyed to **archie** in the From field for the return trip.
compress	Causes the output sent to you to be compressed and uuencoded before being sent.

Command	Description
prog *regexp*	Looks for file names that match *regexp* (regular expression).
site *siteid*	Returns a list of all the files on the server with the specified *siteid*, which can be either a domain name or an IP address.
help	Returns a help guide for mail archie.
list *regexp*	Returns a list of all the servers whose names match *regexp*.
servers	Returns a list of all known archie servers.
whatis *keyword*	Returns a list of possible files that match *keyword* in the **whatis** database. This can then be used in a subsequent mail message with the **prog** command to look up the location of these files.
quit	Terminates processing. Any lines following this command are to be ignored. This is useful if you have a **.signature** file that can be mistaken for commands.

Searching for File Descriptions Using the whatis Database

Hunting for files can be difficult because you can't always tell if you've found the right file. Another type of search that can be used with **archie** is a **whatis** search. A **whatis** search looks up a file name in a software descriptions database. When administrators place files in their ftp archives, they can include an index entry for the file to help others find it and know what the file contains. The index entry creates a relationship between a file name and a set of key words. When you perform a **whatis** search, your search string is used to examine the key word list. Keep in mind that the whatis index is not kept up to date the way the archie index is. The whatis search is performed when you enter the **whatis** command at the archie prompt, as follows:

```
whatis searchstring
```

If the search string is contained in one of the key words, **archie** displays the name of the file and a short description. For example, if you enter **ghostscript** as the search string, **archie** displays

```
ghostscript    The GNU PostScript clone
```

If you've found a description for a file name that sounds appropriate, you can then use **archie** to search and find out where the file is located.

TUNNELING THROUGH THE INTERNET WITH GOPHER

Gopher is a slang term for someone who fetches things for another person, like getting coffee and a prune danish for the boss. On the Internet, **gopher** is a protocol and program that integrates a variety of services into a single application. The **gopher** program makes navigating and using many Internet services and systems as easy as choosing an item from a menu. It searches, retrieves, and displays documents from remote sites on the Internet. The following list contains some types of information you can get using **gopher**.

> **FYI:** There are friendly front-ends for **gopher** if your computer has a dedicated connection to the Internet. The following are popular **gopher** client software programs: **TurboGopher** for the Mac, **PC Gopher II** for DOS, **Xgopher 1.2** for X Window Systems, and the UNIX gopher client for UNIX. All these programs are available via **ftp** at site: **boombox.micro.umn.edu**, directory: **/pub/gopher**.

- Weather forecasts
- Recipes
- Movie reviews
- Computer questions and answers
- Weather maps
- E-mail addresses and phone books for major institutions
- Newspapers and the USENET news
- Electronic copies of literature, such as *Alice's Adventures in Wonderland* and *Moby Dick*
- Library catalogs
- Electronic phone books
- Reference books such as a dictionary and thesaurus
- Jokes and games

Most gopher servers also include links to other servers for browsing and downloading files. Using **gopher** you can access

- Other gopher sites
- ftp sites
- archie file archive databases
- WAIS-distributed database systems
- Gateways to other systems, such as the Cleveland Freenet

FYI: If you're interested in news about gopher servers and software, you can subscribe to the USENET newsgroup **comp.infosystems.gopher** (see Chapter 3 for information on working with newsgroups) or subscribe to the gopher-news mailing list by sending an e-mail message containing the single word **subscribe** to: **gopher-news-request@boombox.micro.umn.edu**. To unsubscribe, send an e-mail message to the same address containing the single word **unsubscribe.**

Getting Started with gopher

Most service providers let you simply type **gopher** to telnet and connect to a gopher site automatically. You can also telnet to a gopher site. Typing **gopher** to make the connection to a gopher site from your service provider is much faster than using **telnet,** and it gives you the option of saving files in your home directory. As is the case for archie servers, crowded conditions exist on gopher servers. The following are the main public gopher client sites.

Host Name	IP#	Login	Area
consultant. micro.umn.edu	134.84.132.4	gopher	University of Minnesota
gopher.uiuc. edu	128.174.33. 160	gopher	University of Illinois
panda.uiowa. edu	128.255.40. 201	panda	University of Iowa

The University of Minnesota **gopher** is the king of all gopher sites. The **gopher** program was originally developed in 1991 by the University of Minnesota to help the campus find answers to computer questions. If typing **gopher** does not automatically connect you to a gopher site, telnet to the University of Minnesota gopher site, by entering

```
telnet consultant.micro.umn.edu
```

and login as **gopher.** If you can't connect to the gopher server, a message appears telling you the connection attempt failed; otherwise, a menu similar to the one in Figure 6-1 appears.

> **FYI:** If you're not using or emulating a VT100 terminal and you are automatically connecting to a gopher site from your service provider, your screen may appear with the characters (B surrounding each item. To display the screen correctly, change your communications software's terminal setting to VT100.

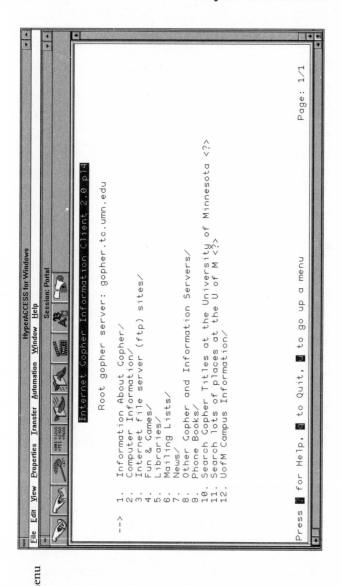

FIGURE 6.1
The gopher menu

Navigating Gopherspace

Once you've started the **gopher** program you're in
gopherspace. The **gopher** program uses a hierarchical menu
structure that resembles a file system. Its menus are analogous to subdirectories (or folders) in a file system. These
submenus can contain files, additional submenus, or other
options, such as telnet sessions, index searches, links to
other servers, and so on. Menu items that contain submenus end with a slash (/). The slash indicates a directory
that is equivalent to another menu level. The <?> denotes
indexed directory resources. Secondary menus that end
with a period indicate text files.

To navigate a menu, enter the number of the menu
item you want and press **Enter** to move to the file or
the next menu level. You can also use the **Up Arrow**
or **Down Arrow** keys to move the pointer to the item
you want, then press **Enter**. After you press **Enter**,
the **gopher** program displays a message indicating it
is making a connection or retrieving the information.
The following are commands for navigating in
gopherspace.

TIP: Anytime you want to see an online summary of the
navigation keys, press **h**.

Command	Action
Enter	View a document
Up Arrow	Move to previous line
Down Arrow	Move to next line
Right Arrow/Enter	Enter or display current item
Left Arrow, u	Exit current item or move up a level
Spacebar, >, +, Pgdn	View next page
b, <, -(hyphen), Pgup	View previous page

Command	Action
n	Go to the line specified by *n*
m	Go back to the main menu
q	Quit with prompt for confirmation
Q	Quit unconditionally
O	Change options
/	Search for an item in the menu
n	Find next search item

> **CAUTION:** As you navigate through gopherspace, you may be incorrectly informed that an item is unavailable. If an item is unavailable, try it again; it may work the second time.

Displaying Information about a Menu Item

The equivalent of the Rosetta stone for deciphering where **gopher** is getting the information for a particular menu item is the equals sign key (=). You use it when you decide you want to make your own connection to that site. For example, you might want to explore an anonymous ftp site yourself to see what other files are available. To return from the technical information back to the menu item, press **Enter**.

Creating Bookmarks to Save Time

Once you have found an item of interest, like any explorer you'll want to mark your spot in gopherspace so you can return to it later. You can only mark your spot in gopherspace if you're using **gopher** directly from your client computer. The **gopher** program is menu based, and moving through menus to get somewhere, especially if you frequently return to a specific menu item, can get tedious. To save you time, **gopher** allows you to mark your spot by creating a bookmark. A bookmark is an item in a customized menu that lets you quickly return to a spot in gopherspace. Using a bookmark returns you to that item, regardless of where you are in **gopher**. Here is how to create a bookmark.

1. At a menu item you want to return to, press **a** to mark the menu item. If you want to add a directory as a menu item, press **A**. A prompt asks you to specify how the bookmark menu item will appear. The title of the menu item is the default text.

2. To create your own text, press **Ctrl-U** and enter the menu text you want.

3. After you create a bookmark menu, press **u** to move up a level, then press **v** to display the bookmark menu. If you want to delete a bookmark or directory menu item, highlight the bookmark menu item and press **d**.

> **FYI:** When you create a bookmark, it's stored in a hidden file named **.gopherrc** in your home directory. The **.gopherrc** file also stores other gopher configurations settings, such as the default terminal emulator to use with **gopher.**

Saving a File Using gopher

The **gopher** program lets you easily grab a file. When you finish viewing a file or press the equal sign key (=), **gopher** displays the following prompt:

```
Press <Return> to continue, <m> to mail, <s> to save
or <p> to print:
```

If you want to save the current item to a file, press **s** and **gopher** displays the Enter save file name: prompt. Enter the name under which you want to save the contents of the item. The file is saved in your home directory. If you are using **telnet** to connect to a gopher site, **gopher** displays the prompt

```
Press <RETURN> to continue, <m> to mail, <D> to
download
```

> **TIP:** If you use a service provider and use **telnet** to connect
> to a gopher site, mail the file instead of downloading it. In
> most cases, downloading a file using **telnet** to connect to a
> gopher site will not work.

Downloading a File to Your Computer. If you're
using a service provider to connect to the Internet and
you want the file on your computer, you need to
download the file from your account to your local computer. In most cases, the **sx** command is used to send a
single file using the XModem protocol. The **sz** command
sends one or more files using the ZModem protocol.
ZModem is faster and can download multiple files. If
your communications software supports the ZModem
protocol use it. To download a file named **pinhead.zip**
from your home directory using the ZModem protocol
to your local computer, enter

```
sz pinhead.zip
```

and issue the command from your local communications
software to receive the file.

Mailing a File Using gopher

You can send the contents of a menu item via e-mail to
yourself or another user. To mail the current item to
yourself, press **m** and **gopher** displays the `Mail Doc-
ument to:` prompt. Enter your Internet e-mail address
to have the contents of the item sent to you by e-mail.

SEARCHING WITH veronica

The **veronica** program is a new service that offers a key
word search of most menu titles in gopherspace. It gets its
name from Very Easy Rodent-Oriented Net-Wide Index to

Computerized Archives. Because **veronica** is accessed through a gopher client, it gives access to all the information available to **gopher** and can connect you directly to the source. The **veronica** program indexes the titles on all levels of the menus for over 300 gopher sites in the Internet.

When **veronica** works, it's a great search tool that will make you glad you took the time to try it. On the downside, **veronica** is a temperamental program. Here are some problems you might encounter when you use the **veronica** program.

- Duplicate items appear from gopher sites pointing to multiple locations of the same information.
- The server names filling your request for information are not identified.
- Some of the menu items appear to be in English, but when you view them, they are in another language.
- Some searches are slow and bound to become slower as more users begin to use **veronica**.
- You may be incorrectly informed that nothing is available, or you may be incorrectly denied access because you are an anonymous user.

Don't let these caveats turn you off to **veronica;** when it works it's sweet. If it doesn't work the first time, try, try, again. Perseverance pays off.

Connecting to veronica

If you're not already connected to a gopher server, type **telnet consultant.micro.umn.edu**, then enter **gopher** at the login prompt. To use **veronica** on University of Minnesota's gopher server, at the main menu choose

```
8. Other Gopher and Information Servers
```

Keep in mind that the menu options and menu numbers may differ from these examples. Choose one of the options to search gopherspace using **veronica**. For example, choose

`2. Search titles in Gopherspace using veronica/`

You can then choose one of the options to search gopherspace using **veronica**. For example, you might choose

`5. Search Gopher Directory Titles at University of`
`Pisa <?>`

This displays `Words to search for:` or a similar prompt. Enter the word you want to search for or press **Ctrl-G** to cancel the search.

Say, for example, you're interested in Microsoft Windows and you want to see what information and files are available for Windows. To start the **veronica** search, enter **windows** as the indexed word to search for. **Veronica** displays a message that it is searching and displays a list of titles matching the index word **windows**.

Understanding the veronica Search Listing

The result of a **veronica** search is an automatically generated gopher menu, customized according to your key word specification. Items on this menu can be taken from many gopher servers. These are functional gopher items (directories and files) that are now accessible via the **gopher** program. Figure 6-2 shows the list that appears after **veronica** is used to search for the indexed word **windows.**

By selecting an item in the menu, you're transparently connected to the **gopher** server on which it is located. For example, if you move to the menu item

`23. ftp.cica.indiana.edu (Largest MS-Windows file`
`collection)/`

pressing **Enter** connects you to **ftp.cica.indiana.edu**. If you connect to **gopher** directly from your client computer and want to access this site again from **gopher**,

FIGURE 6.2

The results of a
veronica search

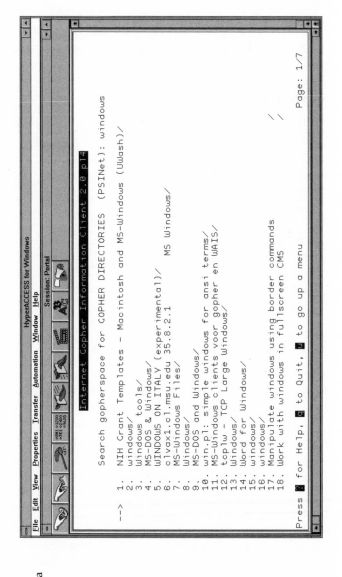

FIGURE 6.2
The results of a
veronica search

you can save the time of navigating through the previous menus by pressing **a** to save the item in your bookmark menu.

Viewing and Downloading Files Using veronica

Menu items that end with a period indicate they're files. If the item is a standard text file such as a news article or FAQ document, selecting and pressing **Enter** displays the file with the **more** paging facility. If the file is a binary file, **veronica** automatically sends the file to your client computer.

> **FYI:** If you are connected to the Internet from a service provider, you will need to download the file from the service provider's computer to your local computer, as explained earlier in this chapter in the section Downloading a File to Your Computer.

SEARCHING DATABASES WITH WAIS

The Internet is rife with databases containing jewels of information. Wide Area Information Servers (WAIS), lets you search through Internet databases looking for articles containing specific words. WAIS (pronounced ways) was developed as method to retrieve information from distributed databases on the Internet through a common interface. There are many different types of databases available; for example, database indexes are built from USENET newsgroup articles, the whois and archie indexes, online library catalogs, and so on. For text documents, every word in the document is usually indexed. A description of a database is known as a *source*, which is noted by the file extension **.src**.

The WAIS program commonly used on Internet with a service provider is actually called SWAIS, which stands for Simple Wide Area Information Server. When you search using a WAIS server, it connects to the server that handles the information you specify. It asks each server to search its index for the word (or words) you specify. The WAIS program searches all the indexed documents in a library and displays documents that match your key word search.

The following list gives you an idea of the types of the sources you can search for using WAIS. Keep in mind that different WAIS programs can display different available sources, and the source databases might or might not include the **.src** extension.

WAIS Source	Description
archie-orst.edu	WAIS-indexed version of archie's anonymous ftp index
au-directory-of-servers	Known servers for WAIS system
bible	King James Bible
Book_of _Mormon	Book of Mormon
clinton-speeches	Bill speaks
college-email	Indexed help guide for finding college e-mail addresses
US-Congress-Phone-Fax	Congressional contact information
domain-organization	Domain name list
hytelnet	Menu-driven version of telnet
internet-phonebook	One-line entries for each person in the WHOIS database (circa 1990)
internet_info	Internet information (Hitch-hiker's Guide to the Internet, Zen and the Art of the Internet, Netiquette, etc.)

WAIS Source	Description
jargon	Dictionary of computing jargon
lyrics	Song lyrics
midi	Technical documents and discussions about MIDI (Musical Instrument Digital Interface)
movie-lists	Archive rec.arts.movies contains lists of references to TV and film credits
movie-reviews	Movie reviews submitted by network newsgroup subscribers
online-libraries-st-george	Complete guide to online library catalogs
poetry	Poems (Brontë, Burns, Byron, Eliot, Frost, Yeats, etc.)
proj-gutenberg	Online books (works of Shakespeare, Lewis Carroll, etc.)
Quran	The Koran
rec.pets	News for the last ten days from the rec.pets newsgroup
recipes	Cooking recipes
roget-thesaurus	Roget's Thesaurus
sf-reviews	Science fiction reviews
supreme.court	Recent supreme court decisions
unix-manuals	UNIX manuals
usenet-addresses	Lists all people who have posted to USENET news groups passing through MIT
US-Budget-1993	The U.S. budget

WAIS Source	Description
uunet	Document explains how to use WAIS to search for files and lists up-to-date software
weather	Weather advisories and earthquake reports
world-factbook	CIA dossier on every country in the world (circa 1990)
wuarcive	Contents of the software archive maintained by Washington University
zipcodes	ZIP code guide

> **FYI:** An excellent annotated subject listing of WAIS sources is available via anonymous **ftp** at site: **ftp.uwo.ca**, directory: **/usr/doc/wais**, file: **src-list.ps** (PostScript format) or **src-list.txt** (ASCII text format).

Starting the swais Program

In most cases, you'll use **telnet** to connect to a WAIS server. To access the **swais** program, at the system prompt type

```
telnet quake.think.com
```

and login as **wais**. If the server **quake.think.com** is busy, enter **telnet nnsc.nsfnet**. The **swais** program will welcome you with the message, Starting swais (this may take a little while)....

> **FYI:** If you have a dedicated connection to the Internet, there are **wais** programs you can use on your computer to access indexed databases directly. For IBM PCs and compatibles the program is **pc-wais**. For the Macintosh the program is **waisstation**. If you're using UNIX and have access to X Windows, try the **xwais** program. These programs are available via **ftp** at site: **quake.think.com**.

Navigating in SWAIS

You can use the **Arrow** keys to move through the source items one at a time. If you know the beginning of the source name you want to search, you can easily move to it by first pressing / (slash). This displays the `Source Name:` prompt; you then enter the source you want to move to. If you plan on accessing the source again, note the number. You can move directly to a source by entering its number. If the Search Sources screen isn't redrawn, or sources you think should be displayed don't appear, press **s** to select new sources and refresh the sources list. To get additional help with navigating **swais**, type a question mark (**?**). If you want to terminate your **swais** connection, type **q**. The following are commands for moving in the Search Sources screen.

Command	Action
j, Down Arrow, Ctrl-N	Move down one source
k, Up Arrow, Ctrl-P	Move up one source
J, Ctrl-V, Ctrl-D	Move down one screen
K, Escape, v, Ctrl-U	Move up one screen
n	Move to source specified by *n*
/*source*	Search for source
v, comma (,)	View current source information
Enter	Perform search

Selecting and Searching Sources

Before making a search using **swais**, you need to select the source items you want to search through. Pressing the **Spacebar** selects an item. For example, move to **recipes** and press the **Spacebar** to select it as the source you want searched. An asterisk (*) appears beside the selection. Pressing **Spacebar** with the highlight on a selected source unselects it. To unselect several sources, press the equal sign key (=).

To begin the search, press **w**. The **swais** program displays the Enter one or more keywords: prompt. Enter the words you want to search for. The **swais** search program is case insensitive, so you don't need to worry about capitalization for your keyword text. It will take a while for the results to be displayed. If you want to move back to the Source Selection screen, press **Ctrl-C**.

Say you want to add a little spice to your life by looking for a recipe for pad thai noodles. Entering the words **pad thai** instructs the server to display a list of documents that contain the words pad thai and display a score telling how appropriate each document is. Figure 6-3 shows the first screen of items matching the key words **pad thai**.

> **FYI:** Not all your searches will be successful. If no matches are found, a bogus message that one item was found appears. The item is actually a listing of the available items in the database.

Viewing and Getting a Selected SWAIS Item

After all the libraries are searched, **swais** displays the titles of the documents that received the highest scores of matches to the search text. The number of documents that the **swais** program displays is limited—usually, between 15 and 50, depending on the WAIS server you're using. You can then select the document you want to view, by using the **Arrow** keys to highlight the one you want and pressing **Enter**. A colon (:) prompt appears at the bottom of the screen. To move to the next page press **Spacebar**.

Let's say that after looking at the document, you decide you want a copy of it. You can send the item to your e-mail address. If you are using a dedicated connection, you can save it to a file. To send the item to your e-mail

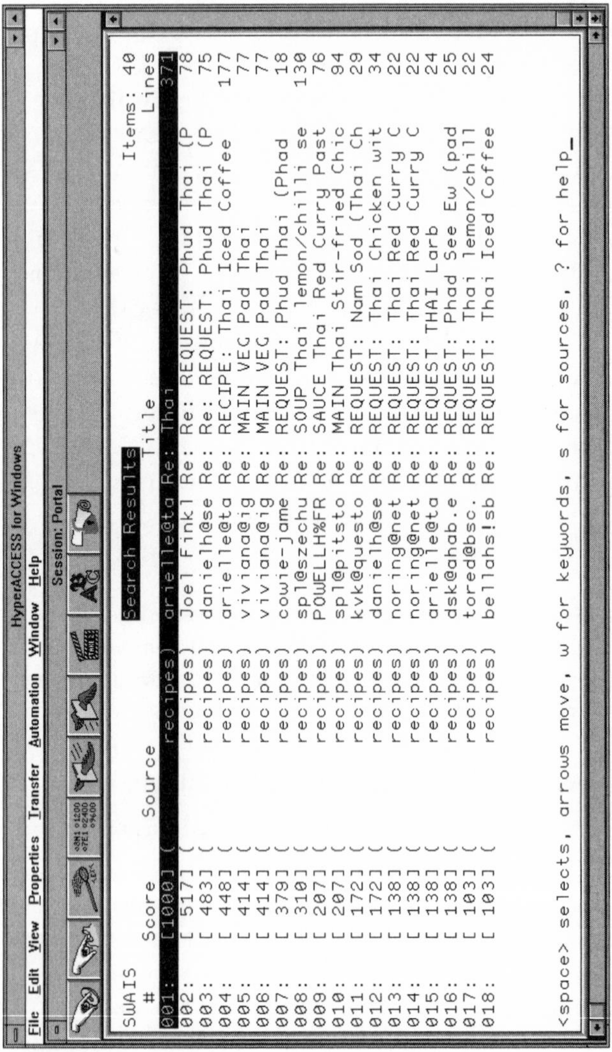

FIGURE 6.3

Items matching a swais search for the key words pad thai

```
File  Edit  View  Properties  Transfer  Automation  Window  Help
                              HyperACCESS for Windows
                              Session: Portal

SWAIS                                                         Items: 40
#      Score    Source                Title                        Lines
001:  [1000]  ( recipes)  ariellle@ta Re: Thai                       371
002:  [ 517]  ( recipes)  Joel Finkl Re: Re: REQUEST: Phud Thai (P    78
003:  [ 483]  ( recipes)  danielh@se Re: Re: REQUEST: Phud Thai (P    75
004:  [ 448]  ( recipes)  ariellle@ta Re: RECIPE: Thai Iced Coffee   177
005:  [ 414]  ( recipes)  viviana@ig Re: MAIN VEG Pad Thai            77
006:  [ 414]  ( recipes)  viviana@ig Re: MAIN VEG Pad Thai            77
007:  [ 379]  ( recipes)  cowie-jame Re: REQUEST: Phud Thai (Phad     18
008:  [ 310]  ( recipes)  spl@szechu Re: SOUP Thai lemon/chilli se   130
009:  [ 207]  ( recipes)  POWELLH%FR Re: SAUCE Thai Red Curry Past    76
010:  [ 207]  ( recipes)  spl@pitsto Re: MAIN Thai Stir-fried Chic    94
011:  [ 172]  ( recipes)  kvk@questo Re: REQUEST: Nam Sod (Thai Ch    29
012:  [ 172]  ( recipes)  danielh@se Re: REQUEST: Thai Chicken wit    34
013:  [ 138]  ( recipes)  noring@net Re: REQUEST: Thai Red Curry C    22
014:  [ 138]  ( recipes)  noring@net Re: REQUEST: Thai Red Curry C    22
015:  [ 138]  ( recipes)  ariellle@ta Re: REQUEST: THAI Larb          24
016:  [ 138]  ( recipes)  dsk@ahab.e Re: REQUEST: Phad See Ew (pad    25
017:  [ 103]  ( recipes)  tored@bsc. Re: REQUEST: Thai lemon/chill    22
018:  [ 103]  ( recipes)  bellahs!sb Re: REQUEST: Thai Iced Coffee    24

<space> selects, arrows move, w for keywords, s for sources, ? for help_
```

address, press **q** then **Enter** to return to the Search Results screen and press **m**. This displays the prompt

Address:

Enter your e-mail address; ^C to cancel

Enter your e-mail address and press **Enter** to send the contents of the item to your e-mail address.

If you are using a dedicated connection and you want to save an item to a file, return to the Search Results screen, highlight the item, and press **S**. A prompt appears asking you to enter the file name. Enter a file name under which to save the file. To cancel the operation, press **Ctrl-C**. If you want to return to the source list, press **q** then **Spacebar**.

WAIS Searches Using gopher

All the functionality of a public SWAIS server can also be accessed through gopher servers. Most gopher servers let you search WAIS databases. For example, you can type gopher (using a service provider) or telnet to the **consultant.micro.umn.edu** gopher server and choose

8. Other Gopher and Information Servers/

The next menu will contain the entry item:

12. WAIS Based Information/

In the next menu, choose

2. List of all WAIS Sources/

This item allows you to perform WAIS searches of all the free sources, but through the gopher interface. The only thing you can't do with this facility is search multiple sources at one time.

USING THE WORLD-WIDE WEB

The World-Wide Web (also known as W^3) merges the techniques of information retrieval and hypertext.

Hypertext is text that is linked together in a nonsequential web of associations that permit you to browse through related topics regardless of the presented order of the topics. Performing a search using the World-Wide Web results in indexed documents containing links to resources such as databases and USENET news.

In order to get the most out of the World-Wide Web, you need to have a direct connection and use client software that supports a graphical user interface running on your computer, such as X Windows, Windows, or the Macintosh. However, the World-Wide Web is also available in text-based versions. A publicly accessible, text-based version of the World-Wide Web is available via **telnet** at **info.cern.ch**.

> **FYI:** World-Wide Web manuals are available via **ftp.** These documents read a little strangely at times because they were generated from online hypertext. To get them, ftp at site: **info.cern.ch**, directory: **/pub/www/doc**, file: **line-mode-guide.txt**.

Chapter 7

UNIX IN ABOUT AN HOUR

Connecting to the Internet thrusts you into the world of the UNIX. The majority of service providers use computers running the UNIX operating system, as do most computers you connect to using **telnet** and **ftp**. If you're a Windows or Mac user, say goodbye to your friendly graphical interface and say hello to the barren UNIX command line. UNIX can be a headache, but this chapter provides relief by giving you quick help with the essential UNIX commands. Take this chapter in small doses as needed.

GETTING STARTED WITH UNIX

Working with UNIX begins with understanding a few essential UNIX concepts, command line fundamentals, and maintenance issues. Getting a grasp on these essentials is sure to save you time and frustration when working with UNIX commands.

The UNIX Shell Game

The most common type of service provider account is called a *shell account*. A shell is the interface between you and the UNIX operating system; it translates commands you enter at the keyboard for the operating system. How the system prompt appears on any UNIX-based computer system depends on the shell that system is using. The three most common UNIX shells are Bourne, Korn, and C. The Bourne shell (**sh**) is on all UNIX systems. The Korn shell (**ksh**) is packed with additional features that go beyond the Bourne shell to make entering and editing commands easier. Both the Bourne shell and Korn shell prompts are usually indicated by a \$. The C shell (**csh**) is a popular shell that provides features similar to the Korn shell's. Its prompt is the %. Most service providers let you switch shells with the shell command (**csh** or **ksh**) at the system prompt.

> **TIP:** Why make things harder than they have to be? If you have your choice of shells, choose the C or Korn shell. The Bourne shell is very limited in features. The C shell is more popular than the Korn shell due to the fact that it was included for free with most versions of UNIX and has been around longer. The Korn shell is now being bundled with many versions of UNIX. Personally we prefer the Korn shell.

Welcome Home

When your shell account is established, you're set up with a home directory. The home directory is your home base on the service provider's computers. It contains all files and directories related to your account. When you create a directory or download files, they are all housed in your home directory.

In addition to regular files, there are *hidden* files in your home directory. Hidden files begin with a period (which is called a dot in this context). Most of your hidden files are files that store configuration settings for programs. Most of these files end with the letters **rc** (run commands). For example, the **.tinrc** file is a configuration file for the **tin** program. Hidden files are excluded from a normal directory listing.

Working on the Command Line

The command line, the space where you enter commands after the system prompt, is your interface to UNIX. Here are some fundamentals for entering and editing commands in this tiny but powerful workspace. If you want to backspace over text and pressing **Backspace** doesn't work, try pressing **Delete**. If that still doesn't work try pressing **Ctrl-H** or **#**. Or if all else fails, press **Ctrl-U** or **@** to erase the entire line.

If you're using the C shell, to save reentering an entire command, press caret (**^**) to identify text to change in a command line. For example, to correct the misspelling of **more** in the line **cat profit.txt |mroe,** at the next prompt, enter **^ro^or**. The C shell repeats the last command and substitutes **or** for **ro**.

The Korn shell uses a different syntax for substituting text. To reexecute the command line and correct the spelling for the previous example using the Korn shell, enter **r ro=or**. You can also reexecute the last command that begins with a specific letter by including the letter of the command after the correction text; for example, **r ro=or c** changes the text and reissues the last command beginning with the letter **c**.

Don't Forget Your history

As the saying goes, history repeats itself, and working with UNIX commands is no exception. Undoubtedly you will need to enter commands over and over again. Both the C shell and the Korn shell store a list of previously issued commands that can be redisplayed on your screen and reexecuted. The last ten or so commands you executed can be displayed by using the **history** command. The C shell lets you identify a previously entered command with an exclamation point (**!**), called a *bang*. For example, using the C shell and entering **!10** repeats the tenth command in the history list. To enter the last command, press **!!**. The C shell also lets you specify a command by a string of characters. For example, **! cd**, reexecutes the most recent **cd** command.

If you're using the Korn shell, you use the **r** (reissue) command. The **r** command by itself repeats the last issued command. Other previous commands can be specified by using **r** and a number; for example, entering **r 5** executes the fifth command in the history list. You can also reexecute a command by specifying the command you want to reissue. For example, **r cat** reexecutes the last **cat** command.

Cleaning Up Your Act

Working with UNIX can lead to screen clutter that detracts from what you're doing. The **clear** command clears the screen and returns the cursor to the upper-left corner. Any time you want to clean up your screen, type **clear**.

Getting Help with man Power

The **man** command displays information about commands from the online reference manuals. Not all systems have the manuals on line, but for those that do, this is a convenient command for getting information for most UNIX commands. Entering **man find**, for example, displays information on the **find** command.

A Command by Any Other Name

The **alias** command lets you define shorthand ways to enter commands. If you're a DOS user you can create aliases for commonly used DOS commands. For example, if you're used to entering the DOS **dir** command to list files, you can create an alias for the UNIX **ls** command that lists files. To do this using the C shell, enter **alias**

dir "ls -al." (Don't enter the period.) If you're using the Korn shell, enter **alias dir="ls -al."** (Don't enter the period.) Entering this **alias** command into your **.cshrc** or **.profile** file makes the alias **dir** available each time you login. This makes **dir** run **ls -a** instead, which lists all the files in the current directory, including hidden files. Entering **alias dir** displays the definition in effect for **dir**. Entering **alias** displays all **alias** definitions in effect. To remove an alias enter **unalias** *alias*.

All Paths Lead to Directories and Files

A path name tells UNIX which paths to take to find a specific directory or file. A path name consists of a directory name or series of directory names separated by slashes (/). The first slash is the root directory, which is at the top of the UNIX hierarchy of file organization. Two types of path names are used in UNIX: absolute and relative. An *absolute* path name always begins with the slash (/), which is the root directory, and lists the file name after the final slash. Using an absolute path always gets you to the specified directory or file, regardless of where you are in the file system.

A *relative* path name describes a path that starts from your current working directory. Relative paths *don't* begin with a slash. Relative path names save you the time of typing a complete path name to access a directory or file beneath the directory you're currently in. A relative path can also use the dot (.) for the current directory or two dots (..) for the parent of the current directory. For example, you can type **cd ..** to change to a directory above your current directory.

WORKING WITH DIRECTORIES

Consider directories your UNIX file cabinet drawers. Files are stored and organized in directories. Every directory and file has a path name. You use directory names in conjunction with UNIX commands to specify the path you want UNIX to apply to a command.

TIP: To save yourself some keystrokes when referring to your home directory in commands, use the tilde (~) or type **$HOME** instead of entering the whole path for your home directory.

Changing Directories

Changing directories is how you get around in UNIX. You change from one directory to another in UNIX systems by using the **cd** command followed by a path name. For example, **cd /tmp** changes to the **/tmp** directory. You can always check what directory you're currently in by entering **pwd**, which stands for print working directory. The path of the directory appears. (In UNIX, the term print usually means display.) If you use the **cd** command by itself without a path name, it returns you to your home directory.

Making or Removing a Directory

The **mkdir** command makes directories in which your files can be stored. Before making a directory, make sure you're in your home directory or a directory under your home directory by using the **cd** command. Enter **mkdir** *directory-name* to create your directory. If you attempt to create a directory with the name of a directory that already exists, a message appears indicating you already have a directory with that name.

The **rmdir** command removes directories. Before using the **rmdir** command you need to remove any files and subdirectories contained in the directory (see Deleting Files later in this chapter), then type **rmdir** *directory-name*. If a directory isn't empty, the **rmdir** command displays an error message.

Copying or Renaming a Directory

The **cp** command used with the **-r** option lets you run off a copy of an entire directory. Entering **cp -r** *directory1* *directory2* copies all the files and any subdirectories of *directory1* into *directory2*. If the directory you want to copy to doesn't already exist, the **cp -r** command creates it.

The **mv** command lets you rename directories. For example, **mv reports business** renames the directory **reports** to **business**. It is a good idea to use the **-i** (inquire) option to have the **mv** command confirm that you want to overwrite an existing directory.

Listing the Contents of a Directory

Reading a directory listing is fundamental. The **ls** command lists the directory and files of the current working directory. Specifying a directory after the **ls** command allows you to list the contents of any directory regardless of the directory you're currently in. For example, **ls ~/download** lists all the files in the **download** subdirectory of your home directory.

Options use the hyphen (-) as the prefix. You can, for instance, list all the subdirectories and hidden files in a directory by entering **ls -a.** You can also include multiple options, for example, to display a long listing that includes subdirectories and hidden files, enter **ls -la.** Here are some useful options for the **ls** command.

Option	Result
-a	Lists all subdirectories and hidden files. Without this option, hidden files — files that begin with a dot (.) — are not listed.
-c	Lists files sorted by creation/modification time.
-l	Displays a long listing of the contents of a directory that includes file permissions, size, and time.
-r	Reverses the order of the sort. By default, lists files in alphabetic order.

Option	Result
-R	Lists the contents of each subdirectory under a specified directory.
-F	Marks directories with a slash (/) and executable files with an asterisk (*). Text files appear without a flag.
-t	Sorts by time of last modification instead of alphabetically, listing most recent first and directories first.

Dealing with Wild Cards

Wild-card characters allow you to specify file names or groups of file names in a directory. These jokers allow you to define a group of files to act on with a given command. For example, the command **ls a*** displays all files beginning with the letter **a**. The * and ? do not match hidden files (files that begin with a dot) unless you explicitly ask for it. If, for example, you want to list only the hidden files in your home directory, enter **ls .***.

WORKING WITH FILES

A file is a storage place for data or executable programs. Everything stored on a UNIX system is in the form of files. The more time you spend on the Internet, the more files you're bound to accumulate. UNIX provides a collection of useful commands for working with files.

What Kind of File Am I?

The **file** command informs you what kind of information a file contains and whether the file is executable, a text file, and so on. You specify the file name of the file you want to know about after the **file** command. For example, entering **file pressure.Z** tells you that the file is a compressed text file. Be aware that the **file** command isn't perfect; it sometimes makes mistakes in identifying files.

Displaying the Contents of a Text File

The **cat** (concatenate) command is a handy file viewer. The **more** command can be used with the **cat** command to display only one screenful of the file at a time. (The **more** command is explained in the following section.) Here are examples of common uses of the **cat** command.

Example	Result
cat *file1*	Displays the contents of *file1*
cat *file1 file2*	Displays the contents of *file1* followed by the contents of *file2*

Displaying a File One Screen at a Time

Displaying a large text file or listing a directory containing numerous files in UNIX causes the text to scroll by at breakneck speed. You can slow down the listing by using the **more** and **pg** commands to display files or directory listings one screenful at a time. Entering **more** *filename* displays the file specified by *filename* one page at a time. You can also pipe (redirect) the output of a command through the **more** command. For example, **ls -al |more** sends the output of the **ls** command to **more**, causing the listing to display one page at a time. Here are the common commands for navigating a file using the **more** command.

Press	Action
Spacebar, Ctrl-D	Displays the next screenful of text
Enter	Displays one more line at the bottom of the screen

Press	Action
q	Quits more
h	Displays the Help screen
lexpr	Searches for *expression*

The **pg** command is similar to the **more** command. When you enter the **pg** command, a colon (:) prompt appears, prompting you to enter display commands. To display the next page, press **Enter**. To get help with the **pg** command, press **h**. To quit displaying a file, press **q**.

Giving the head Command

You can quickly check the first lines of a file to refresh your memory about a file using the **head** command. Entering **head** *filename* displays the first ten lines of the file specified by *filename*; or you can specify the number of lines to be displayed. For example, **head -25 zen.txt** displays the first 25 lines of the file **zen.txt**.

Copying Files

Using the **cp** command lets you clone an exact duplicate of any file. Entering **cp** *file1 file2* copies the contents of *file1* to *file2*. If *file2* does not already exist, it is created; if it does exist, the old contents are overwritten. To ensure that you don't overwrite an existing file, include the **-i** (inquire) option. For example, **cp -i** *file1 file2* prompts for confirmation before overwriting an existing file named *file2*. Pressing **y** confirms that copying should proceed; any other key aborts the **cp** operation. Use the **-p** option to copy the source files and keep the same modification time and permission modes.

Moving and Renaming Files

The **mv** command lets you change the location or names of files. The **mv** command overwrites files that already exist. The command **mv** *file1* *file2* changes the name of *file1* to *file2*. If a file named *file2* already exists, it is replaced with the moved file. To move a file from one directory to another directory you need to include the path. It is a good idea to use the **-i** (inquire) option to ensure that you don't overwrite an existing file. You can also list more than one file to be moved; just be sure the last entry is the directory name that you want to move the files to. For example, **mv profit sales.txt wrksht reports** moves **profit sales.txt wrksht** to the **reports** directory.

Deleting Files

Being a file pack rat can cost you if you're using a service provider. Most service providers charge you for disk space. Why clutter up your home directory with files you don't need? The **rm** (remove) command deletes files. Once a file is deleted, it is gone forever. Because of this, it is a good idea to use the **-i** option, so that **rm** asks you to verify the files it is about to delete. The **-f** option forces the deletion of files without asking you to verify.

Locating Lost Files

The file you want is the file you can't find. If you know at least part of its name, you can use the **find** command to help you locate a lost file. The **find** command is a little more complicated than other commands but its rewards are worth the effort. It lets you find a file by matching characters in a file's name. To find a file, use the following syntax:

```
find pathname expression -print
```

The **find** command searches all files and subdirectories of the directories in *pathname* and checks for files that meet the criteria described by *expression*. The selection criteria in *expression* are checked for each of the files in *pathname*. The criteria are checked until one of them fails, at which point the next file is checked. You can fine-tune the **find** command with options. For example, entering **find. -name "*.txt" -print** displays the path name of all files or subdirectories under the current directory with the file extension **.txt**. The following are some useful options for the **find** command.

Option	Result
-name *filename*	Finds a file if *filename* matches the current file name. An *****, **?**, or **[** and **]** can be used, but must be put within quotes or preceded by a backslash.
-print	Prints the current path name.

Locating Files by Their Contents

Don't have an inkling as to the name of a lost file? Don't give up hope; use the **grep** command. The **grep** command searches the text inside files for a series of characters. Every time it finds a line that contains the specified characters, it displays the line on your screen. If **grep** is looking in more than one file, **grep** displays the name of the file in which the characters occur. The syntax for the **grep** command is

```
grep options "search string" files
```

The *search string* indicates the characters to be looked for. The *files* specifies the files to be searched. If you're searching for a string that consists of more than one word, enclose it in quotation marks. The **grep** program lists the name of the file and the entire line in which it found the search string. If you want to see the file names only, not all the lines **grep** finds, use the **-l** (list) option. If you use the **-i** (ignore case) option, **grep** doesn't distinguish between uppercase and lowercase letters.

If you don't know the exact characters that occur in the file, use **grep's** *regular expressions*. The **grep** program uses the dot (.) as the wild card to search for individual characters. This is equivalent to the question mark (?) wild card used with most other UNIX commands. The asterisk (*) matches any group of characters and behaves as it does with other UNIX commands. To search for a period or an asterisk, precede them with a backslash (\). For example, **grep "report"** * looks through each file in the current directory and displays each file name and every line occurring in the file that contains the word "report."

DO YOU HAVE PERMISSION?

Because UNIX is a multiuser operating system, it includes special built-in safeguards to keep users from accidentally (or even deliberately) deleting one another's directories or files. These safeguards prevent the unauthorized reading, writing, copying, deleting, and executing of files.

Each file has a set of permissions associated with it: *read*, *write*, and *execute*. These three permissions can be applied to the owner (creator) of the file, everyone else on the system, and specified groups of people. Entering the command **ls -l** displays file names and information about their permissions. The permissions are listed, then the number of links (links are special files that point to other files), the owner, the size, the creation date, and finally, the file's name. Here is an example.

```
drwxrwxrwx 8 beavis addwes 4096 Oct 4 16:40 reports
-rwxrwxrwx 12 beavis addwes 4122 Nov 7 17:00 chap1.doc
-rwx------- 12 beavis addwes 4122 Nov 7 17:00 notes.txt
```

The first letter indicates whether the listing is for a directory (d) or a file (-). The next three letters are the permissions given the owner of the file: (r is read or copy permission, w is write or delete permission, x is execute or search permission). The next three letters are the permissions for the assigned groups. The last three letters are the permissions for everyone on the system. The listing shows that **chap1.doc** can be read, written, or executed by anyone on the system. The file **notes.txt** can be read, written, or executed only by the owner, **beavis**.

USING THE MAIL PROGRAM

Electronic mail is the cornerstone of Internet communications. The **mail** and **mailx** are the most widely available UNIX programs for communicating via e-mail. While most systems use **mail**, some systems use the **mailx** program. Both these programs work in a similar manner.

> **FYI:**   The **pine** program is significantly easier to use than **mail** or **mailx**. If you're using a service provider, check to see if the **pine** e-mail program is available. Using Pine is explained in Chapter 2.

Starting mail

When you login to the computer running the **mail** program, the system notifies you if you have e-mail. To read your e-mail, at the system prompt type **mail**. If **mail** is not available, try **mailx**. In some cases, the **mail** program is renamed **Mail**. If you do not have mail, the **mail** program displays the message, No mail for *username*. If you have mail, the **mail** program displays a list of mail headers for the messages waiting to be read, such as

```
mail version X.0 Sat Jun 18 00:20:20:58 PDT 1994
Type ? for help.

"/usr/spool/mail/beavis": 3 messages 2 new 1 unread

>N 1 pnorton Tue Jan 25 16:51 20/619 Cool Idea
for B&B Utilities

N 2 bgates Mon Jan 17 15:55 19/610 Starting
Windows NT
```

```
U 3 pkahn Tue Jan 11 09:08 12/281 Need help with
C++

&
```

Notice that once you enter the **mail** program, the prompt changes from the system prompt to the & prompt. If you're using **mailx**, the prompt is displayed as a question mark (?).

The first line of the mail header list displays the version of the **mail** program you're using and the current date. The second line specifies where your messages will be stored. The mail header list displays information about each message. The following list describes each of the elements, from left to right, in the mail headers list:

Column	Description
Message status	The > character is a pointer indicating the current message. The current message is either the first new message in your mailbox or the last message you read. N (new) indicates the message has just arrived. U (unread) indicates the message was not read before you last quit the mail program. Use **mail's** P (preserved) or **mailx's** H (hold) to indicate that you have read and held the message in your mailbox during the current mail session. An asterisk or an S (saved) indicates that the message has been saved to a file during the current mail session.
Message number	Order in which the message was received.
Sender	Name of the person who sent the message.

Column	Description
Time sent	Date and time the message was sent.
Size	Number of lines and characters in the message (lines/characters).
Subject	Subject of the message.

The header list shows all of your mail headers one screenful at a time. Display the next screenful of mail headers by entering **z**. To display the previous screenful of mail headers, enter **h-** (hyphen). Any time you want to redisplay the mail headers list, enter **h**.

Getting Help in the mail Program

If you enter a question mark (**?**) or **help** at the mail prompt, a list of available commands with descriptions appears. Many of the listed **mail** commands are followed by [message list], a placeholder for the messages you want to affect. If you omit message numbers, the **mail** program affects only the current message.

Reading Your Mail

The **mail** program provides several ways to read your mail. The easiest way is to press **Enter**. To continue reading your messages in sequence, press **Enter** after each message. When you've reached the end of the messages, **mail** responds with the message EOF (end of file), meaning **mail** couldn't find any more mail in your mailbox.

You can also read a specific message by typing the message number at the **mail** prompt (&). For example, pressing **2** displays message number 2, such as:

```
Message 2: From bgates Sat Jun 18 15:55 1994
From bgates (Bill Gates)
Subject: Starting Windows NT How do I start
Windows NT again?
```

If a message is longer than the screen, it quickly scrolls down your screen. Pressing **Ctrl-S** freezes the screen so you can read the message, and pressing **Ctrl-Q** unfreezes the scrolling.

Replying to Mail

When you read a mail message, chances are you will want to reply while the message is fresh in your mind. To send a reply to a message, use the **r** (reply) command. For example, to reply to the author of message number 2, type **r 2** at the **mail** prompt. The **mail** program responds with To: bgates Subject: Re: Starting Windows NT.

The Subject line of the reply automatically inserts Re: and the subject of the original message, so all you have to do is type in your reply. If you like, you can edit the subject line. After completing your reply, press **Enter** to place the cursor on a blank line. Press **Ctrl-D** or type a period, then press **Enter**. The period tells the mail program to send the message.

Depending on how your mail account is set up, the **mail** program might ask if you want to send any carbon copies by displaying a Cc: prompt. If you don't want to send duplicates of the reply to other users, press **Enter**. The reply is sent only to the author of the original message. If you want to send a copy of the message to another user, enter the user's address (*username@address*) at the Cc: prompt.

Managing Your Messages

It's important to keep on top of your e-mail. The **mail** and **mailx** programs let you manage your messages by deleting junk mail, holding on to important messages, and saving messages to files.

The last message you read can be deleted by pressing **d** at the mail prompt. If you accidentally delete a message, restore it by pressing the **u** (undelete) command immediately after the deletion. Once you've read a message, the **mail** program automatically stores the opened message to a storage file, usually named **mbox**. To prevent messages from being moved to your **mbox** file after you read them and quit **mail**, use the **ho** (hold) or **pre** (preserve) command—either command will work. The **h**, **d**, **u**, **ho**, and **pre** commands can be used to affect multiple messages. For example, **d 2, 3, 4** deletes messages 2, 3, and 4, or **d 3-7** deletes messages 3 through 7.

To save the last message you read to a file in your working directory for editing or printing, at the **mail** prompt type **s** *filename*. Until you quit the **mail** program, an asterisk (*) or the letter S appears in the status column, indicating the message has been saved. Any message can be saved by specifying its number from the mail headers list.

The **mbox** file, which is the default storage file for messages you've read, can be opened to allow you to work with the messages it contains by typing **mail -f mbox**. Messages in the **mbox** file can be read, saved, deleted, or replied to using the same commands you use with incoming messages.

> **FYI:** Even if you delete a message and go on to another task in **mail**, you can still save the message from deletion by using the **x** (exit) command, which exits the **mail** program without saving any changes you have made during the current session.

Composing and Sending a Message

Once you know the e-mail address of the person you want to send mail to, follow these steps to compose and send an e-mail message.

1. Type **mail** *username@address*. If you're already in the **mail** program, type **m** or **mail**. To send the same

message to multiple users, separate each address with a space (**mail** *username@address username@address*).

2. Type in the subject of your message at the Subject: prompt.

3. Type in the text of your message. Remember to keep each line around 60 characters in length, so the lines will display correctly on the recipient's terminal.

4. If you decide you don't want to send the message, press **Ctrl-C**. The **mail** program displays the message (Interrupt -- one more time to kill message). Press **Ctrl-C** again to confirm deleting the message.

5. Move the cursor to a new line, press **Ctrl-D** or type a period and press **Enter**. The message EOT (end of text) appears. If a Cc: (carbon copy) prompt appears, enter the e-mail addresses of any other users to whom you want to send copies of the message, then press **Enter**. If you don't want to send a carbon copy, press **Enter**. Your message is sent.

If your mail program doesn't display a carbon copy prompt, on a new line enter **~c** followed by the address (*username@address*) of the user that you want to send the carbon copy to. If you want to send multiple carbon copies, separate each address with a space. The **mail** program also lets you send blind carbon copies, which means the recipient of your message doesn't know that you sent a carbon copy to another user. To send a blind carbon copy, on a new line enter **~b** followed by the user's address (*username@address*).

Including a Message

Why reinvent the wheel — or an existing message for that matter? If another message has text you want to reuse, the **mail** program lets you cut and paste it into your new message. To insert a message into a new message you're composing, use the **~m** or ~**f** command followed by the number of the message to be inserted. If a number is not given, the current message is inserted. The ~**m** command adds a tab character at the beginning of each line of the old message. This is useful when you want to insert text into the new message, for example, to respond to a previous message point by point. Indented lines belong to the original message; the lines that aren't indented indicate your additions. The ~**f** command inserts the old message without tabs, which is useful for including a message that you want to share with another user.

Sending a Text File with mail

The **mail** program lets you stuff a text file into your e-mail and send the contents of the file as though it were a message. To do this, use the following command syntax:

```
mail username@address < textfile
```

where **textfile** is the name of the file you want to send. For example, **mail bevis@shell.portal.com < cool.txt** redirects the contents of the file named **cool.txt** to **beavis**'s mailbox. When you send a file using the redirection symbol (<), **mail** doesn't prompt you for a subject. If you want to add a subject line to the file, add -**s** followed by the text you want added as the subject. If the subject contains spaces, surround your subject text with quotation marks. For example,

```
mail -s "Pyros" beavis@shell.portal.com < cool.txt
```

Sending and Receiving a Binary File with mail

You can't send a binary file through e-mail using **mail** or **mailx**. However UNIX includes the **uuencode** command, which converts a binary file to an ASCII representation, allowing you to send it with your e-mail. Both the sending and receiving computers need to have access to the **uudecode** command or a utility to convert the file. To convert a file named **program.exe** to a file named **ascii.uue,** at the system prompt enter **uuencode program.exe > ascii.uue**. To attach the encoded file to your message, type **~r ascii.uue** in the message area.

When a message containing the encoded file is received, it needs to be decoded using the **uudecode** command. First you need to save the message to a file by entering **s** *filename* to save the message to a file. Because the file has been included in the message, you need to edit out the headers (To, From, Subject, and so on) using a text editor, such as **pico** or **vi**. After editing out the headers, enter **uudecode** *filename*. The decoded program file appears in the current directory.

> **FYI:** Some e-mail systems have limits on the size of any one message, such as 1,000 lines or 50,000 characters. If you run into one of these limits, which can happen when you send files, use the UNIX **split** utility to break a file into multiple pieces and mail them separately. Make sure to tell the recipient to combine the files before the file is converted.

Quitting or Exiting mail

After the **mail** program is started, a working buffer is created in memory where tasks you perform within **mail**, such as moving and deleting messages, are temporarily stored. These changes are stored to disk only when you use the **q** (quit) command. The **q** command moves the messages you've read from your mailbox into a storage file, saves any changes you've made (such as deleting a message), and then quits the **mail** program. If you have unread mail in your mailbox, **mail** displays a message indicating the status of the remaining messages in your mailbox. If you want to exit the **mail** program but not save any changes made during the current session, use the **x** (exit) command. This exits the **mail** program but doesn't save any changes you've made to messages in your mailbox, such as deleting a message.

CREATING AND EDITING FILES WITH PICO

A text editor is an essential tool for working with UNIX. Many programs take for granted that you know how to work with a text editor. For example, **tin** throws you into an editor when you post a message to a newsgroup. The **pico** program is a new generation of UNIX-based text editor. It's an easy-to-use, full-screen text editor that makes working with text files considerably easier than using the standard **vi** text editor. The name **pico** is short for **pi**ne **co**mposer, the text editor included in the **pine** mail program.

Getting Started with pico

To start the **pico** editor and create a file, at your system prompt type **pico**. If you want to edit an existing file, enter **pico** *filename*. If you do not specify a file name, you're asked to supply one when you save a file or exit **pico**. The editing commands, displayed at the bottom of the **pico** screen, are entered by using **Ctrl** key (indicated by the ^ character) and character key combinations.

Getting Help in pico

The **pico** program includes an extensive built-in, context-sensitive help system. So the help text that appears depends on what you're doing at the time you press **Ctrl-G**. Notice that the bottom line changes to show you commands available in help mode. Press **Ctrl-X** to exit the help mode.

Navigating pico

The cursor keys are used to move around the screen. The following are the basic navigation commands.

Press	Moves Cursor
Ctrl-F	Forward a character
Ctrl-B	Backward a character
Ctrl-A	To the beginning of the current line
Ctrl-E	To the end of the current line
Ctrl-N	To the next line
Ctrl-P	To the previous line
Ctrl-V	Forward a page of text
Ctrl-Y	Backward a page of text

Pressing **Ctrl-C** displays where you are in the file. When you press **Ctrl-C,** a message similar to the following appears at the bottom of the screen, centered, and in reverse video: `[line 1 of 1 (100%), character 0 of 0 (0%)]`. This message says that the cursor is located in the first line of the file — and before the first character in the document.

Entering and Editing Text

Entering text is relatively straightforward in **pico**. As you type characters, they are inserted and automatically wrap to the next line. Pressing an **Arrow** key moves the cursor in the indicated direction; pressing **Delete** erases the previous character. The following are **Ctrl**-key combinations that can also be used to delete or undelete text.

Press	Action
Ctrl-D	Delete the character to the right of the cursor
Ctrl-H	Delete the character to the left of the cursor

Press	Action
Ctrl-K	Delete (kill) the entire line at the cursor position
Ctrl-U	Undelete last deleted line or lines at cursor position

You can cut and paste a line of text by pressing **Ctrl-K** to delete the line, which is then stored in a buffer. Move the cursor to the position where you want to insert the deleted line and press **Ctrl-U**. The **pico** program does not have a command to move a block of text in one operation. However, if **Ctrl-K** is used to delete a group of lines one after another with no other commands entered in between, you can paste all the deleted lines back into your text at the location of the cursor, by pressing **Ctrl-U**.

Pressing **Ctrl-J** justifies the current paragraph or, if the cursor is between lines, in the paragraph immediately below it. The **pico** program considers a paragraph to be text that is separated by blank lines, or by lines beginning with a space or a tab. Unjustification can be done immediately after justification by entering **Ctrl-U**.

Checking the Spelling of a File

Spelling errors can distract the reader from the purpose of your document. To check the spelling of a file press **Ctrl-T**. The spelling checker examines all words in the text. It then displays, one at a time, each misspelled word for correction and highlights it in the text. To correct the word, press **Enter** to make your changes. If the word is not misspelled, press **Enter** again to continue the spell check. If a word is misspelled more than once, then you're prompted to confirm the correction of each occurrence of it. Spell checking can be cancelled at any time by entering **Ctrl-C**.

Saving Your Changes

To save your changes, press **Ctrl-O. Pico** displays the message: `File Name to write:`. Enter the name of the file you want to save your changes to. If you're editing a file and your edit session is abnormally terminated, for instance by a telephone line interruption or system crash, **pico** saves the current work to a file. Work is saved under the current file name with the extension **.save**. If the current work is unnamed, it is saved as **pico.save**.

Searching Text

To search for a string of characters in your file, press **Ctrl-W**. You're asked to supply the search string. String searches are case insensitive. A search begins at the current cursor position and wraps back around to check the beginning of your file. The most recent search string is offered as the default in subsequent searches. If the search text is not found, **pico** displays the message `Not found` after your text search.

Inserting a Text File into Your Message

It's often easier to insert an existing file into a message than it is to retype the text. If you want to insert a text file that already exists, press **Ctrl-R**. This displays a prompt asking you to identify the file you want to insert at the current cursor position. The **Ctrl-R** command includes three special options: **Ctrl-G** displays a short help message for the command, **Ctrl-C** cancels the command, and **Ctrl-T** displays the file browser.

Using the File Browser

The **pico** program includes a built-in file browser feature to help you easily navigate directories to search for files. When you press **Ctrl-R** or **Ctrl-O**, the file browser appears as an option labeled ^T (to Files). After you press **Ctrl-T,** the files and directories in your home directory appear. File names, including sizes and names of directories (noted as dir) in the current working directory, are presented for selection. You can move to a specific directory by highlighting a directory and pressing **Enter**. The following are commands for manipulating files in the file browser:

Press	Action
S	Selects the file to be inserted
C	Cancels the file browser
G	Moves to a specific directory
R	Renames files or directories
W	Searches for files
D	Deletes files
M	Makes copies of files

Exiting pico

To exit **pico** and end your editing session, press **Ctrl-X**. If you have not made changes to the file or if you have already saved your changes, you're returned to your system prompt. If changes have been made but not saved, you're prompted as follows: Modified buffer: Save before leaving (y/n)? If you press **y**, the name of the file you are editing is displayed after the prompt File Name to write:. If you want to change the name of the file, supply a new name. In the event you use the name of an existing file, you're warned that the file exists and asked if you want to overwrite the existing file.

CREATING AND EDITING FILES WITH VI

The **vi** (visual) editor is the best text editor ever developed . . . NOT! The only reason for the existence of the

vi editor today is the burden of history. It's the one editor included in virtually all versions of UNIX. Most UNIX users have been raised on **vi** editor and old habits die hard. In case you're using a system that doesn't provide a friendlier text editor like **pico**, here is an introduction to **vi**.

Getting Started with vi

To create or modify an existing file using **vi**, type **vi** *filename* at the system prompt. A file name can be up to 256 characters in length and can include any characters except special characters (such as **-, *, ?, <, >,** /). To start **vi** without specifying a file name, type **vi**. You can give the file a name later when you exit **vi**.

The tilde (~) characters that appear at the far left of the screen after you execute **vi** indicate empty lines. The line at the bottom of the screen is called the *status line*. The status line shows the file name and the number of lines and characters in the file. Once you fill the screen with text or move the cursor to the end of the file, the status line disappears. If you start **vi** to create a new file without a file name, no status line is displayed. To bring up the status line, press **Ctrl-G**, which displays a new status line.

Command and Insert Modes

The **vi** editor operates in two modes, the command mode and the insert mode. The *command mode* allows you to enter commands for performing a wide range of **vi** functions, such as cursor movement and editing operations. When you start **vi**, you're in the command mode. The *insert mode* allows you to enter text into a file. The **vi** program doesn't indicate which mode you're in, but pressing **Esc** always places you in the command mode. You leave the command mode and enter the insert mode by pressing **i** (insert) in the command mode. Remember, if you try to type a command

while you're in the insert mode, the command characters are inserted as text. Press **Esc** any time you want to
exit the insert mode and enter another command.

Working with vi Commands

The **vi** program is command intensive; there is a command for everything, right down to moving the cursor
one space. Most **vi** commands consist of one or two
letters and an optional number, with uppercase and
lowercase versions that usually perform related but different functions. For example, pressing **x** deletes the
character at the cursor; pressing **X** deletes the character
preceding the cursor. You don't need to press **Enter** after
entering most **vi** commands. However, commands pre-
ceded by a colon do require you to press **Enter** after the
command. For example, to use the command **:q!** to quit
vi and abandon changes, you must press **Enter** after
pressing the exclamation point. Most **vi** commands let
you add a repeat factor, which multiples the number of
units of text the command affects.

Most **vi** editing commands can also be combined with
movement commands and repeat factors to further
improve your productivity. If you want to repeat an
editing command, you can save time by pressing the
repeat command (**.**) instead of retyping the command.
To repeat a command, position the cursor where you
want to repeat the command and type a period (**.**). Keep
in mind that you can repeat only the last editing command you execute and that this command doesn't work
with cursor movement or scrolling commands.

If you enter an incorrect **vi** command, it can be
undone by using an undo command immediately after
the incorrect command is entered. (The insert mode
command (**i**) is an exception; if you mistakenly enter
this command, press **Esc** to return to the command
mode.) The **u** command undoes the last edit. The **U**

command undoes edits on a single line, as long as the cursor remains on that line.

Units of Text in vi

Many **vi** commands affect specific units of text, such as characters, words, lines, sentences, and paragraphs. The following is a list of the characters used to indicate different units of text when **vi** commands are issued. These commands are used with another command. For example, **d(** deletes back to the beginning of the current sentence.

Press	Unit of Text Affected
w	To the beginning of the next word, not including punctuation
W	To the beginning of the next word, including punctuation
b	To beginning of the current word, not including punctuation
B	To beginning of the current word, including punctuation
$	End of current line
O	Beginning of current line
(	Back to beginning of current sentence
)	Ahead to beginning of next sentence
{	Back to beginning of current paragraph
}	Ahead to beginning of next paragraph
H	Home position at the upper-left corner of the screen
M	Beginning of the middle line of the screen
L	Beginning of the last line on the screen

Moving the Cursor

The **vi** program includes a lot of commands for moving through an entire file. However, you can't move the cursor below a tilde (~), which indicates a line without text or spaces, tabs, or returns. With most cursor movement commands you can specify the number of times you want the cursor movement repeated. You can't use a repeat factor on any **Ctrl** commands, such as **Ctrl-D**, which scrolls the screen down, or on any commands that position the cursor at a specific point on the screen. The following list contains **vi** editor cursor movement and scrolling commands.

Press	Moves
Spacebar, l (lowercase L)	Right (forward) one character position
h	Left (backward) one character
+	First character of next line
- (hyphen)	First character of previous line
Down Arrow, j	Same position in line below
Up Arrow, k	Same position in line above
G	Last line in work buffer
nG	Move to line number n
Ctrl-D	Down half screen
Ctrl-U	Up half screen
Ctrl-F	Forward almost a full screen
Ctrl-B	Backward almost a full screen
Ctrl-E	Down one line at a time
Ctrl-Y	Up one line at a time
Z	Up or down a screen, leaving cursor on same line
z	Moves the current line to the center of the screen
z-	Moves the current line to the bottom of the screen

> **TIP:** In **vi**, each line in a file is assigned a sequential line number. Line numbers, by default, are not displayed. To display line numbering, enter the command **:set nu**. Only lines that include text are assigned numbers.

Inserting and Appending Text

The **vi** program includes several commands for inserting text into a file. All these commands are executed from insert mode. To enter insert mode, first position the cursor at the location you want to insert text, then in command mode type **i**. You're now ready to begin entering text at the cursor location. The characters you type appear to the left or before the cursor position and push any following characters to the right. Pressing **Enter** creates a new line at any point while you're entering text. Here is a list of commands to insert or append text to a file.

Press	Action
i	Inserts before cursor
I	Inserts before first nonblank character on line
a	Appends after cursor
A	Appends at end of line
o	Opens a line next line down
O	Opens a line next line up

Deleting and Replacing Text

The **vi** editor provides a complete set of delete commands. Delete commands are performed in the command mode. You can include a repeat factor in these delete commands to delete a number of characters or words. The number is placed following the **d** but preceding either the **w** (words) or **b** (characters, backward); for example, typing **d4w** deletes the next four words. After executing a delete command, **vi** remains in the command mode. Keep in mind that the **u** (undo) command, as explained earlier, is particularly useful in undoing deletion commands. The following lists and explains **vi** editor delete commands.

Command	Deletes
x	Character at cursor.
X	Character before cursor.
dd	The line in which the cursor is currently located.
d*unit*	The specified *unit* of text. Add a number before the *units* to specify the more than one unit to delete; for example **d5b** deletes five characters backward.
d Enter	Two lines, current and following.
dG	To end of the file.
d1G	To beginning of the file.

The **vi** editor lets you overtype text, so that you don't have to delete and then enter new text. The **r** replace command allows you to replace the character at the cursor, and the **R** command lets you replace characters until you press **Esc**.

Joining Two Lines

The **vi** program lets you merge shorter lines to form a longer line with the **J** (join) command. To join two lines, first position the cursor anywhere on the first line, then type **J** to merge it with the line below it. The repeat command can be used to merge consecutive lines into one line.

Searching for Text

The **vi** program lets you search through a file for specified strings of characters. Search commands search your file for a specified pattern. When a match is found, you can make changes and then search for the next occurrence of the string. A forward search proceeds from the cursor to the end of the file and a backward search proceeds from the cursor to the beginning of the file. If you begin in the middle of a file, therefore, the search does not cover the entire file. The following list contains **vi** search commands.

Command	Result
/pattern	Searches forward in file
?pattern	Searches backward in file
n	Finds next pattern in same direction
N	Find next pattern in opposite direction

Searching and Replacing Text

The **vi** editor provides a powerful tool for searching and replacing text entries. With one command you can automatically replace a string of characters, such as a consistently misspelled word, wherever it occurs in the file. The replacement command syntax is

`:%s/old_pattern/new_pattern/`

Once a replacement command is entered, **vi** checks each line of a file for a given pattern. When the pattern is found, **vi** automatically replaces the old pattern with the new pattern you've specified. For example, suppose you want to search through your file and find each occurrence of the word **Internet** and change it to **Cyberspace**. Type **:%s/Internet/Cyberspace** then press **Enter**. If **vi** doesn't find any matches, it responds with the message Substitute pattern match failed.

Keeping It Clean

Once you start making extensive changes to your file, the screen can get cluttered with leftover command symbols before **vi** redraws your screen. Redrawing a screen means updating the screen to reflect your changes and removing command symbols that have been executed. Because the **vi** editor redraws the screen only periodically, you may need to clean up the screen by pressing **Ctrl-L.**

Recovering from a System Crash

If the system crashes while you're editing a file with **vi**, you can recover text that was not saved to disk before the crash. After the system is restored and the system prompt appears, type **vi -r** *filename* where *filename* is the name of the file you were working on when the system crashed. The displayed file reflects the changes you made, but did not save, before the system crash. Use the **:w** (write) command immediately to save the salvaged copy of the work buffer to disk; then you can continue to edit the file.

Exiting vi

When you're creating or editing a file, you're actually working on a copy of the file that is stored in a *work buffer*, an area temporarily set aside in memory. Any changes you make to a file using **vi** affect only the file in the buffer until you instruct **vi** to save your file to disk. In other words, your edits don't affect your original file until you save your work.

You can exit **vi** and abandon any changes you've made by not saving the contents of the work buffer. To quit **vi**, you must be in the command mode. Use **:w** (write) frequently during a work session to prevent loss of your work in the event of a system crash.

Command	Action
Shift-ZZ	Saves your changes to a file and exits vi.
:x	Saves your file and exits vi.
:w	Writes (saves) the buffer contents to the disk but doesn't exit vi.
:w *filename*	Saves your work to another file, but continues to edit the same file. If you started vi without a file name, this names the file being edited.
:q!	Quits vi without saving your changes.
:q	Quits vi if you haven't made any edits to the file; otherwise, prompts you with, No write since last change (:quit! overrides).

COMPRESSING FILES

Compressed files save disk space and transfer time. If you're using a service provider, this translates into cold cash by saving you connect time and storage fees. Two programs widely used for compacting your files are **compress** and **pack**. The **compress** command reduces the storage size of a file by use of a compression algorithm (Lempel-Ziv). When you compress a file, it is replaced by a file with a **.Z** extension. Typically the **.Z** file is about half the size of the source file. The amount compression depends greatly upon the contents of the input file. To restore a compressed file, use the command **uncompress**. Given a file, **report.text**, with a size of 4608 bytes, entering **compress report.text** results in a file **report.text.Z** with a size of 2696 bytes. To uncompress **report.text.Z**, enter **uncompress report.text**. Note that with the **uncompress** command the **.Z** extension is optional. To display the percentage of reduction, add the **-v** option. This displays the percentage of reduction effected by **compress**.

The **pack** command is an older UNIX command that compacts files and replaces them with compressed files with a **.z** appended to the file name. To restore the files to their original form, use the **unpack** command. Entering **pack part1.ps**, compacts **part1.ps** replacing **part1.ps** with a compressed file, and appends **.z** to the file name. To unpack a previously packed file named **mucho.z**, enter **unpack mucho.z**.

Viewing a Compressed File

To view a compressed file without changing the contents of the **.Z** file, use the **zcat** command. Unfortunately you can't view **.z** files. The **zcat** *filename* command is like the **cat** command except it displays uncompressed output for the contents of a compressed file (compressed files end with **.Z**). It leaves the compressed file unchanged. Entering **zcat readme.Z** displays the compressed contents of the file **readme.Z** in an uncompressed format.

WORKING WITH ARCHIVE FILES

Most PC and Macintosh users share files by running down the hall with a disk, otherwise known as *sneakernet*. UNIX users, on the other hand, rarely access a floppy disk drive. In many cases, files are stored (backed up) to tapes and floppies using one of three commands: **tar** (tape archive), **cpio** (copy in or out), and **pax** (portable archive exchange). It is unlikely that you will encounter **cpio** archive files on the Internet. Most archived files that are stored in the **tar** format can be restored using the command **tar xvf** *filename,* where *filename* is the name of the archived files.

Many sites combine and compress files using the UNIX **tar** and **compress** commands. Remember, files compressed with the **compress** command end with a **.Z**. To decompress a file that ends with **.tar.Z,** first use the **uncompress** command (**uncompress** *filename***.tar.Z**).

This uncompresses the file and removes the **.Z** extension. You can then enter the command **tar xvf** *filename*.**tar** to unarchive the file.

CAN WE TALK?

The **talk** command establishes CB-like communications between two users; 10-4 good buddy! It allows users to send messages back and forth interactively. For example, entering **talk beavis** displays the following on the **beavis@netcom.com** terminal:

```
Message from Talk_Daemon@netcom at 2:03-talk:
connection requested by butt-head@netcom.com
talk: respond with: talk butt-head@netcom.com
```

where **netcom.com** is your computer's host name and **butt-head** is your user name. The other user (in this case **beavis)** then enters **talk butt-head**. This establishes the link between the terminals and displays a line across the middle of the screen. Both Beavis and Butt-Head can now type messages on the screen at the same time. The text appears as it is typed. The text each user writes appears in the top half of the screen. The other user's text appears in the bottom half of the screen. You can redraw the screen at any time while using the **talk** command by pressing **Ctrl-I.** To exit, enter **Ctrl-C** or **Ctrl-O**.

Appendix

Getting a Dial-up Connection to the Internet

There are many paths to the Internet for the lone IBM PC or Mac surfer. A growing number of dial-up connection options and service providers confronts anyone wanting access to the Internet. Costs and types of service vary greatly. Determining the best service provider for you depends on a variety of factors. In this appendix, we arm you with the information you need to choose the service provider that is right for you.

BEFORE YOU START SHOPPING

Before you can make a connection to a service provider, you must have a modem and communications software installed on your computer. Your modem determines the speed with which you interact with the service provider. In modem communications speed is everything. If you're working with a 2400-bps modem, upgrade if you can. The expense of buying a faster modem will quickly be paid back by money you save in hourly connection charges, especially if you plan to download and upload files.

TYPES OF INTERNET ACCESS

There is a growing number of service providers offering connections to the Internet, which breaks down into three main types of access available options.

■ The shell account, the most common type of dial-up connection, gives you a UNIX account on the service provider's computer and usually gives you access to the full range of Internet services, such as e-mail, network news, **telnet,** and **ftp.**

■ Menu-based connections are easier to use than shell accounts but are less versatile. These types of accounts are good for the users who want built-in hand-holding. Menu-based accounts can limit service options, but some offer the full range of Internet services. Several major online services are setting up options for access to Internet services that use a menu-based format. For example, Delphi Communications and BIX both offer menu-based access to the Internet.

■ E-mail-only connections are available from most major online and e-mail services, such as America Online, CompuServe, and MCI Mail. This type of Internet connection is limited to sending and receiving mail on the Internet.

FYI: If you're using a UNIX computer, some service providers let you connect to the Internet via UUCP communication software. This is an excellent option for a small business because it gives the business an Internet domain address and lets the business set up its own user accounts. With this type of connection, you can get e-mail and news in batches instead of paying for a more expensive, dedicated connection.

THE COST OF GETTING THERE

Finding an economical way to dial up and connect to a service provider is a major concern. Long-distance telephone charges can easily exceed your costs for connect time on the computer. When choosing a service provider, evaluate the cost of connecting to its system as part of the cost of using the service.

Every service provider offers a local number at its site for local direct dial up. If you live in the local area of that service provider, your telephone charges can be zero or minimal. Some service providers offer an 800 telephone number for access but add a surcharge to their hourly charges.

Many service providers offer local numbers in major cities or areas they consider to be their prime territory. These numbers link you to a Public Data Network (PDN) that handles your telecommunications at cheaper rates than those of regular telephone companies. The PDN rates vary depending on the time you call and where you call from. The rates are usually highest during busy weekdays, while nights and weekends are the cheapest.

In most cases, you won't need to have your own PDN account because service providers offer PDN services at a discount through the service provider. However, if you're connecting to a service provider that doesn't offer its own PDN package, you may want to set up your own PDN account. Keep in mind that having your own PDN account involves an extra step of having to dial the PDN to connect to your service provider.

> **FYI:** PC Pursuit is a U.S. Sprint service that provides flat-rate off-hours dial-up services to cities all over the United States. Users pay a one-time registration fee that covers 30 hours of non-prime-time use. Excess hours are billed at a low monthly rate. Call (800) 736-1130 for more information.

SERVICE PROVIDER CHECKLIST

Choosing a service provider requires some thought as to your needs and costs. Here is a checklist of things to keep in mind when you shop for a service provider.

- What types of accounts does the service provider offer?
- Does the service provider offer all the basic Internet services (e-mail, news, **telnet,** and **ftp**)? Some service providers charge à la carte for some services. For example,

they may not include telnet or ftp service in the basic charge but offer it for an additional hourly charge.

- What are the sign-up charges? Many service providers charge a one-time sign-up fee. Some are high to discourage low-volume customers.

- What is the basic monthly service charge? Most providers charge a basic monthly fee, but some don't, charging a minimum usage fee instead.

- What are the hourly connection charges for the service? Don't confuse this charge with telecommunications charges, which are often billed in addition to the hourly service charge. Some service providers charge different hourly rates for busy times versus off times, while others use one flat hourly rate regardless of the time. Some service providers don't charge by the hour but charge a flat rate.

- How much storage space are you allotted for files and e-mail? Many service providers charge you for disk space beyond a minimum amount allotted for your account.

- What modem speed are you and the service provider using? Some service providers charge different hourly rates depending on the modem speed you're using. For example, a 2400-bps modem might have a cheaper hourly rate than a 9600-bps modem, but it may cost you more in telecommunication charges because it takes longer to download a file to your computer.

- What are the telecommunications charges to connect to the service provider? Remember, these charges can be higher than the connection charges.

- Does the service provider provide technical and customer support either via e-mail or over the telephone?

SERVICE PROVIDERS

The following is a listing of service providers that offer affordable accounts for individual users. If you already have a modem and communications software, many service providers allow you to login to their systems as a guest to check them out. E-mail addresses are included in case you can already communicate via e-mail.

> **FYI:** If you know someone who has access to the Internet, ask him or her to get a text file that provides an extensive listing of service providers for individual access to the Internet available via anonymous **ftp** at site: **liberty.uc.wlu.edu**, directory: **/pub/lawlib**, file: **internet.access**. This text file also lists BBSs that offer Internet connection services. BBSs are all over the map, and chances are there may be one in your local calling area.

a2i communications
1211 Park Avenue #202
San Jose, CA 95132
Voice: (408) 293-8078 (voice mail)
Dialup: (408) 293-9010; login as **guest**
E-mail: info@rahul.net

BIX
1030 Massachusetts Avenue
Cambridge, MA 02138
Voice: (800) 695-4775
Dialup: (800) 695-4882; login as **bix,** Name: **bix.internet**
E-mail: bix@genvid.com

Colorado Supernet, Inc. (CSN)
Colorado School of Mines
1500 Illinois Street
Golden, CO 80401
Voice: (303) 273-3471
E-mail: info@csn.org

CONCERT
Communications for North Carolina Education Research and Technology
3021 Cornwallis Road

Research Triangle Park, NC 27709
Voice: (919) 248-1404
E-mail: jrr@concert.net

CRL

Box 326
Larkspur, CA 94977
Voice: (415) 381-2800
E-mail: support@crl.com

DELPHI

1030 Massachusetts Avenue
Cambridge, MA 02138
Voice: (800) 544-4005
Dialup: (800) 365-4636; login **JOINDELPHI**, password: **INTERNETSIG**
E-mail: walthowe@delphi.com

CERFnet

P.O. Box 85608
San Diego, CA 92186
Voice: (800) 876-2373
E-mail: help@cerf.net

HoloNet

Information Access Technologies, Inc.
46 Shattuck Square, Suite 11
Berkeley, CA 94704
Voice: (510) 704-0160
Dialup: (800) NET-HOLO (lists local numbers); enter local access number, login: **guest**
E-mail: info@holonet.net

The IDS World Network

InteleCom Data Systems
11 Franklin Road
East Greenwich, RI 02818
Voice: (401) 884-7856
Dialup: (401) 884-9002, (401)785-1067

E-mail: sysadmin@ids.net

JVNCnet

6 von Neuman Hall
Princeton University
Princeton, NJ 08544
Voice: (609) 258-2400
E-mail: market@jvnc.net

MSEN

628 Brooks Street
Ann Arbor, MI 48103
Voice: (313) 998-4562
E-mail: info@msen.com

NETCOM Online Communication Services

4000 Moorpark Avenue, No. 209
San Jose, CA 95117
Voice: (408) 554-UNIX
Dialup: (800) 488-2558 (lists local numbers); enter
local access number, login: **guest**
E-mail: info@netcom.com

NovaLink

P.O. Box 11
Shrewsbury, MA 01545
Voice: (800) 274-2814
E-mail: infor@novalink.com

NYSERNet

111 College Place Room 3-211
Syracuse, NY 13244
Voice: (315) 443-4120
E-mail: luckett@nysernet.org

OARnet

Ohio Supercomputer Center
1224 Kinnear Road
Columbus, OH 43212
Voice: (614) 292-8100

E-mail: nic@oar.net

Pathways

1903 Broderick Street #4
San Francisco, CA 94115
Voice: (800) 758-4777, (415) 346-4188
Dialup: (415) 474-3813; login: **pathways**, password:
demo
E-mail: info@path.net

Performance Systems International, Inc.

11800 Sunrise Valley Drive, Suite 1100
Reston, VA 22091
Voice: (800) 82 PSI 82
E-mail: all-info@psi.com or gds-info@psi.com

Portal Communications Company

20863 Stevens Creek Boulevard, Suite 200
Cupertino, CA 95014
Voice: (408) 973-9111
Dialup: (408) 725-0561; login: **new**, **info**, or **help**
E-mail: info@portal.com

PREPnet

305 S. Craig Street, 2nd Floor
Pittsburgh, PA 15213
Voice: (412) 268-7870
E-mail: prepnett@andrew.cmu.edu

THEnet Texas Higher Education

Network Information Center
Austin, TX 78712
Voice: (512) 471-2444
E-mail: info@nic.the.net

VERnet

Academic Computing Center
Gilmer Hall
University of Virginia
Charlottesville, VA 22903

Voice: (804) 924-0616

E-mail: jaj@virginia.edu

The WELL (Whole Earth 'Lectronic Link)

27 Gate 5 Road

Sausalito, CA 94965

Voice: (415) 332-4335

Dialup: (415) 332-6106; login: **newuser**

E-mail: info@well.sf.ca.us

The World Software Tool and Die

1330 Beacon Street

Brookline, MA 02146

Voice: (617) 739-0202

Dialup: (617) 739-9753; login: **new**

E-mail: office@world.std.com

Index

! (bang) (C shell), 155

A

a2i communications service provider, 195

Abbreviations, common expressions (table), 15–16

Account
  id, 5
  menu, 8
  shell, 8

Addresses
  address book, managing,
    44–48
  Internet
    characteristics, 3
    service providers, 195–199

Alias, 44

alias command, 156

America Online, addressing
  e-mail to, 30

Anonymous ftp sites, *E* FTP (File
  Transfer Protocol)

AppleLink, addressing e-mail to,
  30

archie program, 12. *See also*
  Information retrieval
  connecting to directly, 127
  with e-mail, 130–132
  with telnet, 126
  list of servers (table), 126
  locating files with, 125
  modifiers (table), 129
  setting the search type (table),
    127

Articles (in newsgroup threads).
  See also Newsgroups
  displaying, 69
  encrypting and decrypting, 72
  marking as read and unread,
    71
  navigating, 71
  posting followup and base, 81
  replying to, 81
  saving, 75
  searching for, 72
  selecting, 73–74

ASCII files, transferring, 116. *See
  also* Files

ATTMail, addressing e-mail to, 30

B

Backing up, files, 188. *See also*
  Disaster recovery

Bang (!) (C shell), 155

BBS (bulletin board systems),
  accessing with telnet, 90,
  92

Bcc: field (pine program), 29

Binary files. *See also* Files
  receiving, with mail program,
    172
  saving, 76
  sending with mail program, 172

BITNET
  addressing e-mail to, 30
  news, accessing, 85

BIX
  addressing e-mail to, 30
  service provider, 195

Catch the Addison-Wesley
Online Wave

Coming soon from the authors of
The Instant Internet Guide:

The Elements of E-Mail Style
A Guide to Writing Concise and Effective Electronic Mail
by David Angell and Brent Heslop
0-201-62709-4   224 pages

Available in May 1994

Related titles:

The Internet Companion
A Beginner's Guide to Global Networking
by Tracy LaQuey with Jeanne C. Ryer
0-201-62224-6   208 pages

The Internet Companion Plus
A Beginner's Start-up Kit for Global Networking
by Tracy LaQuey with Jeanne C. Ryer
0-201-62719-1   208 pages
Includes free Internet access software

The Online User's Encyclopedia
Bulletin Boards and Beyond
by Bernard Aboba
0-201-62214-9   832 pages